Simple Animals

John Stidworthy

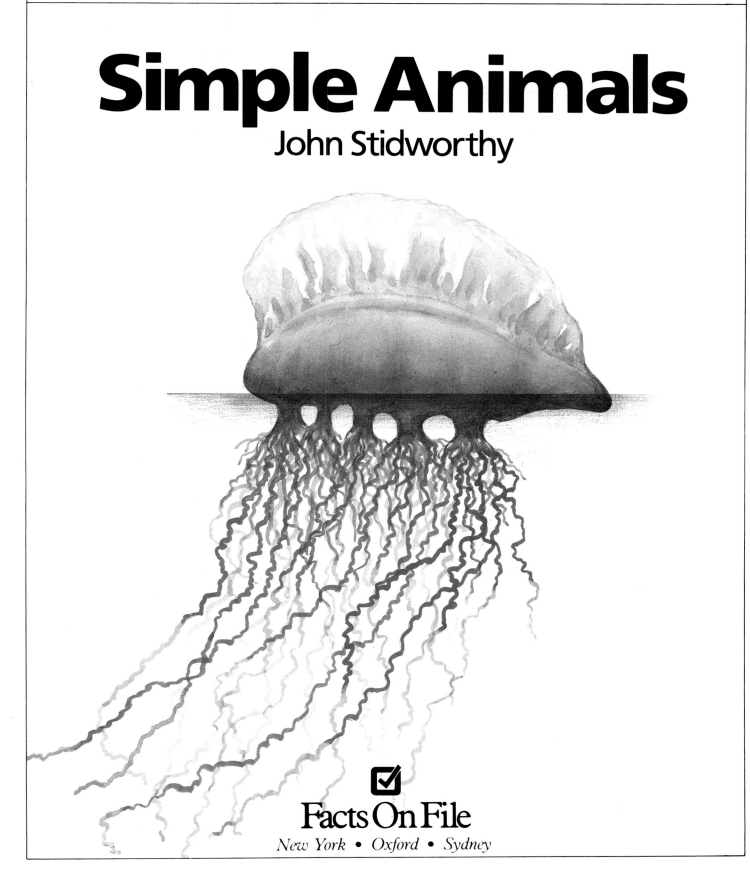

Facts On File

New York • Oxford • Sydney

SIMPLE ANIMALS
The Encyclopedia of the Animal World

Managing Editor: Lionel Bender
Art Editor: Ben White
Designer: Malcolm Smythe
Text Editor: Madeleine Samuel
Project Editor: Graham Bateman
Production: Clive Sparling, Joanna
   Turner

Media conversion and typesetting:
   Robert and Peter MacDonald,
   Una Macnamara

AN EQUINOX BOOK

Planned and produced by:
Equinox (Oxford) Limited,
Musterlin House, Jordan Hill Road,
Oxford OX2 8DP

Prepared by Lionheart Books

Library of Congress
Cataloging-in-Publication Data
Stidworthy, John. 1943-
   Simple animals/ John Stidworthy
   p   cm.——(Encyclopedia of the Animal
   World)
   Bibliography: p.
   Includes index
   Summary: Introduces the invertebrate
animals which include protozoa, sponges,
crabs, and octopuses.

1. Invertebrates – Dictionaries – Juvenile
literature.
[1. Invertebrates.] I. Title II. Series

QL362.S85 1989   592 - dc20
89-35005 CIP AC

ISBN 0-8160-1968-1

Published in North America by
Facts On File, Inc.,
460 Park Avenue South,
New York, N.Y. 10016

Origination by Alpha Reprographics Ltd.
Perivale, Middx, England

Printed in Italy.

10 9 8 7 6 5 4 3 2 1

FACT PANEL: Key to symbols denoting general features of animals

SYMBOLS WITH NO WORDS

Activity time

● Nocturnal

● Daytime

◐ Dawn/Dusk

◉ All the time

Young/adult comparison

▢ Young like adults

▭ Young unlike adults

◨ Likeness of young to adults
   varies with species

Conservation status

☠ All species threatened

☗ Some species threatened

No species threatened (no symbol)

SYMBOLS NEXT TO HEADINGS

Habitat

◣ General – land/sea

● Grassland

≈ Sea

◉ Fresh water

≈ Fresh and/or Sea water

◉ Parasitic

Diet

■ Other animals

■ Plants

◨ Animals and Plants

CONTENTS

PREFACE

The National Wildlife Federation

For the wildlife of the world, 1936 was a very big year. That's when the National Wildlife Federation formed to help conserve the millions of species of animals and plants that call Earth their home. In trying to do such an important job, the Federation has grown to be the largest conservation group of its kind.

Today, plants and animals face more dangers than ever before. As the human population grows and takes over more and more land, the wild places of the world disappear. As people produce more and more chemicals and cars and other products to make life better for themselves, the environment often becomes worse for wildlife.

But there is some good news. Many animals are better off today than when the National Wildlife Federation began. Alligators, wild turkeys, deer, wood ducks, and others are thriving – thanks to the hard work of everyone who cares about wildlife.

The Federation's number one job has always been education. We teach kids the wonders of nature through *Your Big Backyard* and *Ranger Rick* magazines and our annual National Wildlife Week celebration. We teach grown-ups the importance of a clean environment through *National Wildlife* and *International Wildlife* magazines. And we help teachers teach about wildlife with our environmental education activity series called *Naturescope*.

The National Wildlife Federation is nearly five million people, all working as one. We all know that by helping wildlife, we are also helping ourselves. Together we have helped pass laws that have cleaned up our air and water, protected endangered species, and left grand old forests standing tall.

You can help too. Every time you plant a bush that becomes a home to a butterfly, every time you help clean a lake or river of trash, every time you walk instead of asking for a ride in a car – you are part of the wildlife team.

You are also doing your part by learning all you can about the wildlife of the world. That's why the National Wildlife Federation is happy to help bring you this Encyclopedia. We hope you enjoy it.

Jay D. Hair, President
National Wildlife Federation

INTRODUCTION

The *Encyclopedia of the Animal World* surveys the main groups and species of animals alive today. Written by a team of specialists, it includes the most current information and the newest ideas on animal behavior and survival. The Encyclopedia looks at how the shape and form of an animal reflect its life-style – the ways in which a creature's size, color, feeding methods and defenses have all evolved in relationship to a particular diet, climate and habitat. Discussed also are the ways in which human activities often disrupt natural ecosystems and threaten the survival of many species.

In this Encyclopedia the animals are grouped on the basis of their body structure and their evolution from common ancestors. Thus, there are single volumes or groups of volumes on mammals, birds, reptiles and amphibians, fish, insects and so on. Within these major categories, the animals are grouped according to their feeding habits or general life-styles. Because there is so much information on the animals in two of these major categories, there are four volumes devoted to mammals (*The Small Plant-Eaters; The Hunters; The Large Plant-Eaters; Primates, Insect-Eaters and Baleen Whales*) and three to birds (*The Waterbirds; The Aerial Hunters; The Plant- and Seed-Eaters*).

This volume, *Simple Animals*, includes entries on protozoans, sponges, jellyfish, earthworms, ragworms, crabs, lobsters, starfish, sea urchins, octopuses, squids and lancelets. Together they number almost 250,000 species. They are all animals without backbones (invertebrates) that live in the sea, fresh water or moist land habitats. They also include many parasites – creatures that feed on the tissues of others without killing them. The watery environment of these species comprises the body fluids (blood, digested food) of their hosts. (Those invertebrates that live mainly on land, the insects, spiders and their allies, are dealt with in a separate volume, *Insects and Spiders*.)

The animals dealt with in *Simple Animals* are referred to as "simple" only because their basic body plan and organization are often not as intricate or highly developed as those of other animals, such as fish, amphibians, reptiles, birds and mammals. Yet they show an immense range of shapes, sizes and life-styles. Some, such as the common pond animals Amoeba and Hydra, are only just visible to the naked eye. Others, for example the Giant squid, can grow to 60ft in length. Many, like slugs, move about a lot, while others, such as barnacles, are attached to a rock or even to the bottom of ships throughout their adult life. Most slugs, snails and worms are plant-eaters. Crabs, lobsters, cuttlefish, squids and starfish are meat-eaters. Mussels, clams, fan worms and sea anemones collect or filter tiny particles of food – animal or plant – from the water. For complexity of structure and intelligence, the squids and octopuses come near to rivaling the fish in expertise in their mastery of the water and in their behavior.

Each article in this Encyclopedia is devoted to an individual species or group of closely related species. The text starts with a short scene-setting story that highlights one or more of the animal's unique features. It then continues with details of the most interesting aspects of the animal's physical features and abilities, diet and feeding behavior, and general life-style. It also covers conservation and the animal's relationships with people.

A fact panel provides easy reference to the main features of distribution (natural, not introductions to other areas by humans), habitat, diet, size, color and breeding. (An explanation of the color-coded symbols is given on page 2 of the book.) The panel also includes a list of the common and scientific (Latin) names of species mentioned in the main text and photo captions. For species illustrated in major artwork panels but not described elsewhere, the names are given in the caption accompanying the artwork. In such illustrations, animals are shown to scale unless otherwise stated; actual dimensions may be found in the text. To help the reader quickly determine the type of animal each article deals with, in the upper right part of the page at the beginning of an article is a simple line drawing of one or more representative species.

Many species of animal are threatened with extinction as a result of human activities. In this Encyclopedia the following terms are used to show the status of a species as defined by the International Union for the Conservation of Nature and Natural Resources:

Endangered – in danger of extinction unless their habitat is no longer destroyed and they are not hunted by people.

Vulnerable – likely to become endangered in the near future.

Rare – exist in small numbers but neither endangered nor vulnerable at present.

A glossary provides definitions of technical terms used in the book. A common name and scientific (Latin) name index provide easy access to text and illustrations.

WHAT IS AN INVERTEBRATE?

An invertebrate is any animal that lacks a backbone, or vertebral column. Worms, snails, crabs, insects, squids, sea anemones – these and many other familiar animals are all invertebrates. They comprise over 95 percent of the more than a million known species of animal.

DIVERSE DESIGNS

Apart from lacking a backbone, many of the invertebrates have little in common. They range in size from microscopic animals like the amoeba to giant squids that are 18 million times longer. They include animals as different as desert locusts and jellyfish. They live all over the world, from the

▶Animals can be divided in 39 main groups, or phyla. Here some of the groups are arranged in a sequence with the simplest animals at the bottom, and the more complicated at the top.

▼Myriads of invertebrate animals drift in waters of the seas. This sample seen under a microscope includes crab larvae, other crustaceans, and tiny jellyfish that are feeding on them.

VERTEBRATES
(For example Mammals, Birds, Reptiles, Fish)

LANCELETS & SEA SQUIRTS

ECHINODERMS

MOLLUSKS

INSECTS AND MYRIAPODS

ARACHNIDS

CRUSTACEANS

SEGMENTED WORMS

FLATWORMS

NEMATODES & OTHER WORMS

COELENTERATES

SPONGES

PROTOZOANS PROTISTS

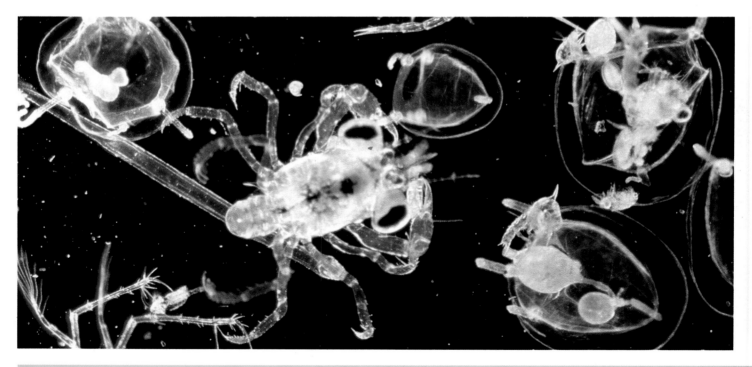

ocean depths to the mountaintops, at the polar ice-caps and in the air.

Life started in the seas, and almost all the main groups (or phyla – there are 39 of them) of invertebrates have marine species. Fewer, just 14 phyla, have representatives in fresh water. Only the jointed-legged invertebrates – insects, spiders and their allies – have truly conquered dry land.

Many invertebrates are free-living, that is, they can move around by themselves. Numerous others live attached to something else for most of their lives, such as the barnacles attached to a rock. Some invertebrates are pests that feed on our crops. Many species are parasites, living on or in people, or other animals or plants.

Some do great damage and are difficult for doctors or farmers to combat. On the other hand, many invertebrates are very useful. These include the earthworms that constantly turn over the soil and make land fertile, and species ranging from octopuses to crabs and prawns, which many of us consider are good to eat.

TRENDS IN EVOLUTION

The first life forms we know of are fossils of simple single-celled creatures like bacteria. These are found in rocks as much as 4 billion years old. Much later simple plants and animals evolved. Not until rocks from 600 million years ago do we find animals with shells or any other hard parts. From

then until the present time, many kinds of animals have evolved. Some have long since died out, while others still continue as today's living species.

The main trend in animal evolution has been towards a more complicated and more "efficient" body, with better organization and more sophisticated senses and brains. However, there are numerous animals that have hardly changed for millions of years. Their bodies are obviously well suited to their particular way of life.

ANIMAL GROUPS

Animals can be divided into major groups (phyla) on the basis of their body plans. It is possible to draw up a sort of "scorecard" of groups, from

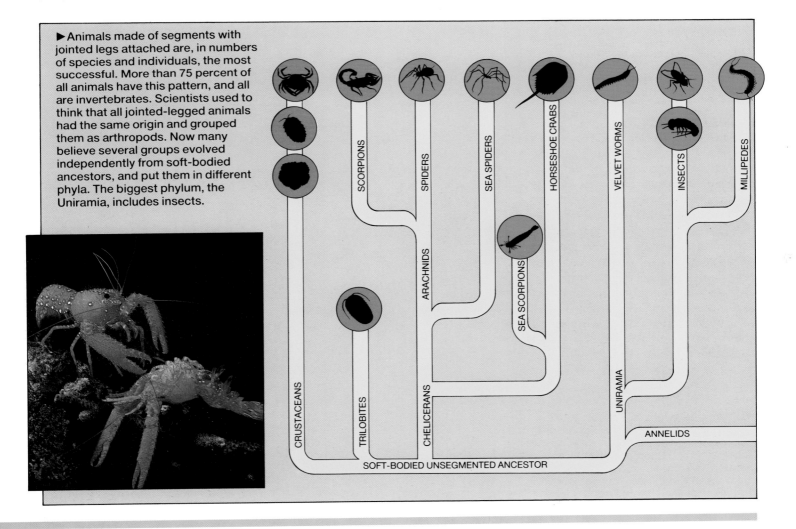

▶ Animals made of segments with jointed legs attached are, in numbers of species and individuals, the most successful. More than 75 percent of all animals have this pattern, and all are invertebrates. Scientists used to think that all jointed-legged animals had the same origin and grouped them as arthropods. Now many believe several groups evolved independently from soft-bodied ancestors, and put them in different phyla. The biggest phylum, the Uniramia, includes insects.

SCORPIONS

SPIDERS

SEA SPIDERS

HORSESHOE CRABS

VELVET WORMS

INSECTS

MILLIPEDES

ARACHNIDS

SEA SCORPIONS

CRUSTACEANS

TRILOBITES

CHELICERANS

UNIRAMIA

ANNELIDS

SOFT-BODIED UNSEGMENTED ANCESTOR

the simplest animals at the bottom to the more advanced at the top.

An attempt can also be made to draw an evolutionary tree; this is a diagram that shows which group another group or groups has evolved from. This is not so easy to do for invertebrate groups since these soft-bodied animals are rarely preserved as fossils. Although we can trace the rough outlines of evolution, we may have to do much detective work on the living species to fill in the details.

Evidence for the detection may come from the body plans of different groups. For example, those groups that have segmented bodies, such as the annelids and crustaceans, may all have had the same ancestor way back. Additional evidence may come from the development of individuals of different groups from egg to adult. They may have larval stages that are identical, as do many marine species of mollusc and worm, although the adults look very different.

CELLS AND LAYERS

The simplest invertebrates consist of a single cell. All other animals are made of many cells working together. The simplest of these are animals such as sponges, which consist of a single layer of cells with little difference in the jobs each does. One stage more complicated are the jellyfish and sea anemones, which have two layers of cells. Some of the cells perform discrete and different functions and form tissues such as muscles or nerves.

"Higher" animals (including many invertebrates and all vertebrates) are constructed of three basic cell layers. In these animals, clumps of highly

▶ Different body plans. The amoeba (top photo) is a single cell that carries out all life processes. The cuttlefish, snail and lancelet (bottom photo) have many cells grouped into organs for particular jobs. The lancelet *Amphioxus* is segmented, the cuttlefish and snail are not.

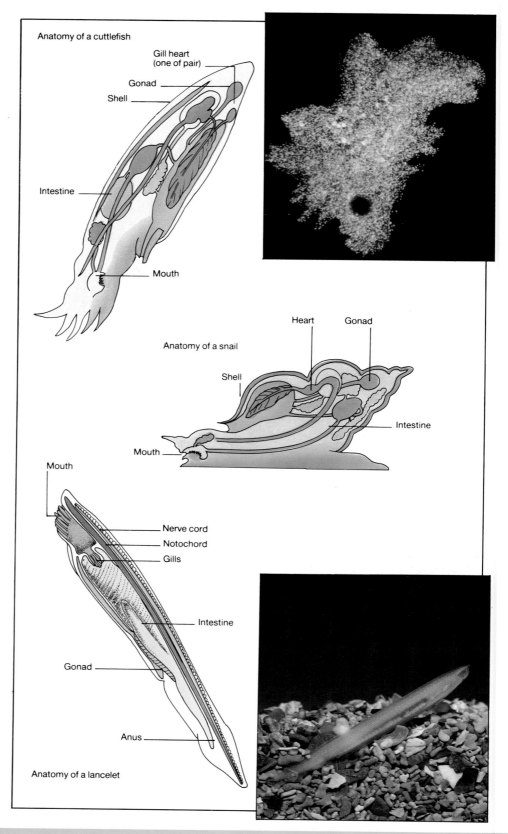

Anatomy of a cuttlefish

Gill heart (one of pair)
Gonad
Shell
Intestine
Mouth

Anatomy of a snail

Heart
Gonad
Shell
Intestine
Mouth

Mouth
Nerve cord
Notochord
Gills
Intestine
Gonad
Anus

Anatomy of a lancelet

specialized cells form organs like the liver and the heart.

Among the three-layered animals further divisions can be made. The more advanced animals develop a special space in the body, called the coelom, as they grow and mature. Within those with coeloms, there is a split between two different ways this cavity forms. In most invertebrates, the coelom develops as pockets from the gut. In chordates (vertebrates and relations) and in the echinoderms (spiny-skinned invertebrates) it develops by a splitting of the middle cell layer (the mesoderm). The two latter groups also both have an internal skeleton of calcium compounds.

IN TWOS OR IN FIVES

One of the most obvious differences separating some invertebrate phyla is

▶ Many invertebrates are solitary animals, like this giant millipede. It feeds, moves and lives separately from others of its kind. Millipedes only come together for mating. (Millipedes, insects and spiders are dealt with in a separate volume.)

▼ Invertebrates like these moss animals live in colonies. In these colonies, a skeleton is produced and lived in by a large number of individuals. Here it may be difficult to tell whether the animal seen is one individual or a colony of individuals.

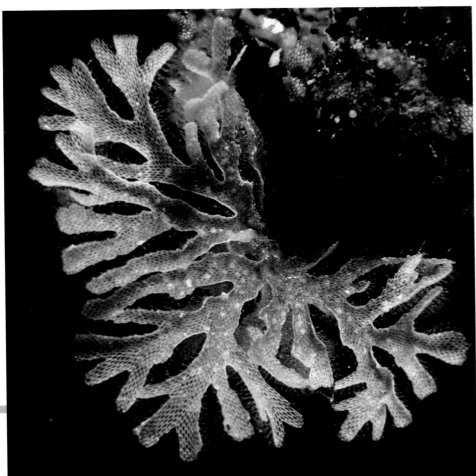

the overall appearance of the body. The majority of animals are bilaterally symmetrical – they have two halves that are mirror images. At the front is a head, at the back a tail. From worms to slugs to lobsters, this is typical. Cut them from head to tail and you get two equal halves. For animals that are highly mobile, it is a useful arrangement. The body can develop to move efficiently in one direction, and the head can have special organs, such as eyes and taste receptors, to investigate what the animal is moving towards.

Some phyla, though, are radially symmetrical, with bodies similar in all directions around the vertical. Cut them in half in any direction and you get equal halves, as with a starfish. This is perhaps ideal for an animal that is fixed to one spot, such as a sea anemone, or drifts passively with the current, like a jellyfish. Its food and enemies are just as likely to come from one direction as another.

PROTOZOANS

On the bottom of a pond a hunt in miniature is carried out. A microscopic animal has blundered into an amoeba. It is trapped. Slowly the amoeba changes shape, and "arms" of its body ooze around its prey. It surrounds the animal, making a special compartment for it. The amoeba begins to digest its quarry, but is ready to make other captures if it can.

Protozoans are tiny. Some resemble amoeba and feed in an animal-like way on other small organisms. Others have a parasitic way of life, living inside a host and feeding on the host's tissues, fluids or gut contents. Yet a third type are plant-like, having the green pigment chlorophyll and being able to use the Sun's energy to make their own food – as do true plants.

All these organisms are different enough from other animals to be put in their own kingdom, Protista, and different enough from one another to be divided into seven main groups. What all have in common is that they are single-celled, and they are minute.

MICROSCOPIC WORLD
The largest of the protozoans, such as some big amoebas, or *Volvox*, are 1/20in or so across – big enough to be seen with the naked eye. But most protozoans are much smaller, and can only be seen with a high-power microscope.

Protozoans are found almost everywhere. Their main need is for water to live in. They are found in both fresh and sea water. Being so small, there is enough water for them to live in the thin films of moisture covering soil particles and some plants.

Habitats ranging from the ice fields of polar regions to hot springs with water at 155°F are home to some sort of protozoan. They have even been found at depths of 13,000ft in the sea.

PROTOZOANS Kingdom Protista (*about 31,000 species*)

○ □

■ Habitat: water, damp places; some parasitic in other animals.

▨ Diet: animals, plants, organic matter. Some make their own food by photosynthesis.

Breeding: usually reproduce asexually by splitting of the cell.

Distribution: worldwide.

Size: less than 1/20in across.

Color: mostly colorless.

▼▶ Species of protozoan In *Volvox* (1) many individuals form a ball-like colony. *Vorticella* (2) stays attached to a support. *Difflugia* (3) makes a shell of tiny sand grains. *Spirostomum* (4) swims propelled by its hair-like cilia. *Stentor* (5) is trumpet-shaped. *Amoeba* (6) changes shape as it moves. *Actinosphaerium* (7) rolls along by shortening and lengthening its spreading "rays." *Arcella* (8) crawls beneath its shell, putting out several false feet or pseudopodia.

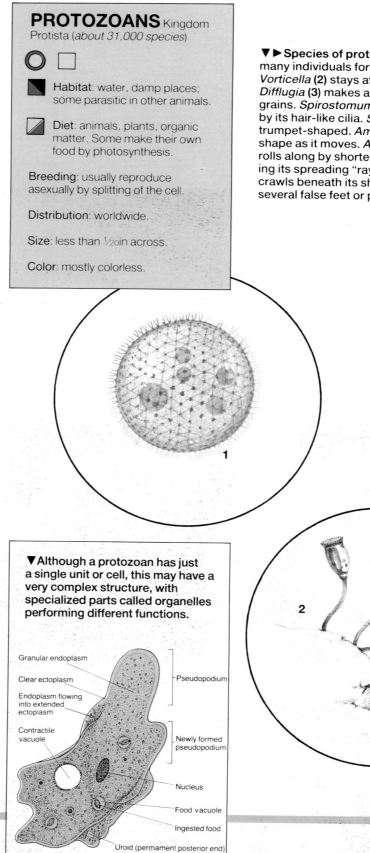

▼Although a protozoan has just a single unit or cell, this may have a very complex structure, with specialized parts called organelles performing different functions.

Granular endoplasm

Clear ectoplasm

Endoplasm flowing into extended ectoplasm

Contractile vacuole

Pseudopodium

Newly formed pseudopodium

Nucleus

Food vacuole

Ingested food

Uroid (permanent posterior end)

ALL IN ONE

In protozoans, a single cell has to carry out all the processes of life – feeding, movement, regulating water content, reproducing and so on. These are carried out in other organisms by special groups of cells or multicellular organs. So the protozoan single cell is by no means "simple." Often different parts can be distinguished within the cell, each of which does a particular job. The nucleus is the organizer, or control center. There may be special food vacuoles in which food is held and digested. Water vacuoles may fill with excess water, and then shrink as this is expelled from the cell.

KILLER LIFE-STYLES

Five of the main groups of protozoan, comprising about 6,000 species, contain organisms that live inside other animals and plants. These parasites include some dangerous disease organisms, such as those that cause coccidiosis in birds, and malaria in humans. In Africa, about one million people die each year from malaria, and in warm climates as a whole, millions more suffer from the disease.

The malaria parasite, *Plasmodium*, reproduces inside a mosquito. When the insect bites a human, the person becomes infected. Each *Plasmodium* enters a red blood cell. There it feeds and grows. Then it divides to produce many new individuals. The red blood cell breaks, and they are released. Every one of them can infect another blood cell. As many blood cells are infected, vast numbers of parasites are released at the same time. They produce a fever at regular intervals, which is highly characteristic of malaria. A mosquito sucking the infected blood transmits the disease onwards.

Other fatal diseases caused by protozoans include sleeping sickness. The organism concerned, *Trypanosoma*, is carried from one human to another by the Tsetse fly.

VARIED FORMS

Among the free-living protozoans there are three main types. The first, the amoebas, include some forms with no fixed shape, and many which have shells around their single cell. Amoebas move about by putting out pseudopodia (false feet), which are flowing extensions of the cell.

The flagellates, the second type, are protozoans which move using a whip-like flagellum. Some of these contain chlorophyll. Third are the ciliates, which seem in many ways the most complex of protozoans. Unlike the others, they have a special mouth region. They have many short cilia (hairs) covering the body.

WHIPPING ALONG

Both flagella and cilia have a similar internal make-up of tiny tubules, but cilia are shorter. Cilia are present in organisms right through the animal world and have a uniform structure.

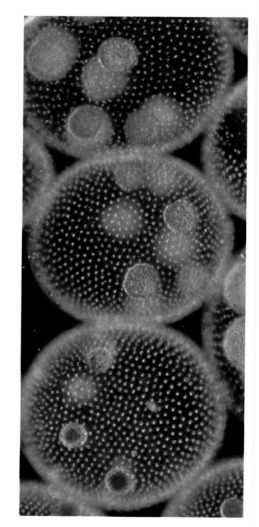

▶ Inside a *Volvox* colony, dark spheres representing new colonies forming, can often be seen. *Volvox* is green because it contains chlorophyll using which it can make its own food in the same way as plants.

▼ Shapes of protozoan *Actinophrys* (1), a Sun animalcule. *Opalina* (2), with many nuclei. *Acineta* (3), which traps prey on its sticky tentacles. *Elphidium* (4), with a shell. *Euglena* (5) moves with a whip-like flagellum, as does *Trypanosoma* (6), a parasite. *Hexacontium* (7) has an elaborate shell.

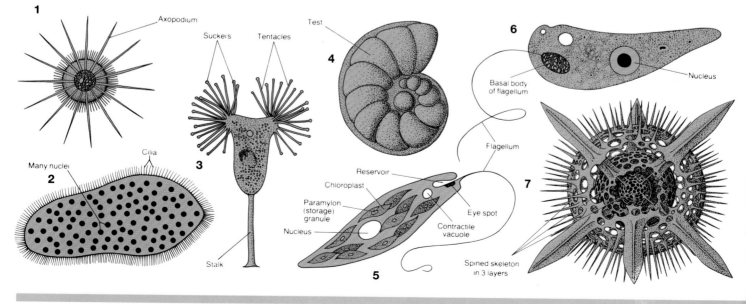

Even the cilia that line our own breathing tubes are built in the same way as those of protozoans.

In ciliates there may be hundreds of cilia. They are arranged in rows, and they beat in waves in a regular pattern. Some ciliates can travel distances of $1/20$in or more in a second. This may not sound much, but in relation to their length, or viewed down a microscope, it seems very fast indeed.

Not all ciliates are swimmers. Some, such as *Stentor* and *Vorticella*, stay attached to a support by their base, and use rings of cilia around their mouth to capture food. Several species of ciliate play an important part in breaking down human waste materials in sewage beds. Others are important for large plant-eating animals such as cows. Ciliates live in their gut, and help break down plant cell walls that the cow cannot digest by itself.

DIVIDE AND MULTIPLY
A few ciliates go through a process that resembles sexual reproduction in multicellular organisms. This involves

▲Long thin filaments stick out through the shell of a *Globigerinoides* species. They are used to trap food and for movement.

the fusion of a "male" and a "female" cell. But most protozoans reproduce by simply splitting in two. In suitable conditions their numbers may build up fast. Amoebas have no fixed way of splitting, but flagellates usually divide lengthways along the cell, and ciliates across the cell, after duplicating the mouth region.

SPONGES

From a small boat in the Mediterranean a skin diver is working. He goes overboard and swims down to the rocky seabed. He searches for a while and then tears up an oddly shaped lump. He seems unable to find anything else of interest and returns to the boat with his prize. He is doing something that has been done for thousands of years in the area – fishing for bath sponges.

▶ A portion of the Great Barrier Reef off Australia shows blue sponges with many holes or pores encrusting the coral limestone alongside other animals.

The sponge used in the bath is really just a skeleton. Once gathered from the seabed, a sponge is left to dry in the Sun until the soft parts have rotted away. Bath sponges have relatively soft skeletons, made of tough protein. Other types of sponge have harder skeletons, made of rods and stars of minerals such as silica.

ALL SHAPES AND COLORS

Sponges may be globular, fan- or vase- shaped, or tall thin tubes. They may branch, or form massive clumps.

Some exist as just a thin crust on hard rock on the deep seabed.

Whatever its shape, the body plan and functioning of a sponge are the same. The sponge draws in water through many small pores in its surface. It expels the water through one large opening, usually at the top. Cavities inside the sponge are lined with cells that have flagella. These waft the water through the animal. Around the flagellum of each cell is a fringed collar that traps tiny food particles that the cell then absorbs. Oxygen is

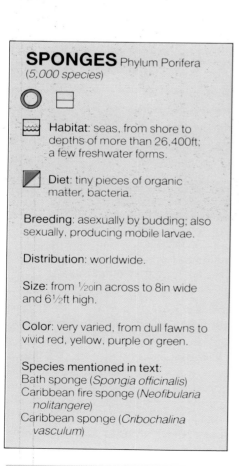

SPONGES Phylum Porifera
(5,000 species)

Habitat: seas, from shore to depths of more than 26,400ft; a few freshwater forms.

Diet: tiny pieces of organic matter, bacteria.

Breeding: asexually by budding; also sexually, producing mobile larvae.

Distribution: worldwide.

Size: from 1/20in across to 8in wide and 6½ft high.

Color: very varied, from dull fawns to vivid red, yellow, purple or green.

Species mentioned in text:
Bath sponge (*Spongia officinalis*)
Caribbean fire sponge (*Neofibularia nolitangere*)
Caribbean sponge (*Cribochalina vasculum*)

absorbed from the water and waste materials carried away.

Sponges come in many different colors, although some kinds are drab. They may be bright green because of plant-like algae living in them.

DARK AND WET

Sponges occur from low on the sea-shore to the ocean depths. They cannot withstand drying out. On the shore, they are most likely to be found in places where they are sheltered from the Sun by a rock overhang. They thrive in dark places where plants cannot survive. Most grow attached to hard rock but a few live on sand or mud. One small group is found in freshwater lakes and rivers.

ENEMIES AND DEFENSES

Sea slugs graze on sponges, and some turtles, fish and starfish nibble them. Unable to move away, sponges such as the big Caribbean sponge have developed poisonous chemicals as a defense. Poisons may also keep the sponge's surface clean by stopping other animals settling or growing over them. If touched, the Caribbean fire sponge gives a severe burning sensation that lasts for several hours.

REPRODUCTION

Sponges can reproduce by forming outgrowths that separate from the parent (budding) or by pieces breaking off. Some produce special resting buds called gemmules. Freshwater sponges die off in winter, but the gemmules survive to start new growth in the spring. Sponges also reproduce sexually. Larvae are produced that swim or creep about before finding a place to settle and grow to an adult.

◄The columns of the sponge *Aplysina lacunosa* rise from the seabed. A large opening through which the sponge pushes out water can be seen on the top of the front column.

SEA ANEMONES, JELLYFISH

It is a sunny day in summer and the sea is deep blue. Children paddling watch a dinner-plate sized transparent jellyfish as it slowly pulsates near the surface. Once their eyes have become used to looking in the water, they notice that there is not one but a whole swarm of Common jellyfish. In each circular body, four horseshoe-shaped purple blobs mark the animal's reproductive organs.

The jellyfish is basically a bell-shaped animal with a mouth in the middle underneath. The fringe of the bell carries stinging tentacles. The mouth opens into a space inside the body where food is digested. The body has two skin-like layers of cells with jelly in between.

A sea anemone is built to a similar plan, but is upside down compared to a jellyfish. It spends most of its time anchored to the seabed, and is tubular rather than bell-shaped. Again, it has a mouth surrounded by stinging tentacles, leading into the hollow body. The sea anemone type of body is known as a polyp.

SEA ANEMONES, JELLYFISH Phylum Cnidaria
(about 5,400 species)

○ ⊟ 🏊

〰 **Habitat:** seas, free-swimming or bottom-dwelling, from tidal zone to ocean depths; small number of freshwater species.

■ **Diet:** capture other animals up to size of fish; some filter particles of food from the water.

Breeding: very varied, but both sexual and asexual. Some species alternate between two forms in their life history – free swimming sexual jellyfish (medusa) and sedentary asexual polyp.

Distribution: worldwide.

Size: from about 1/20in to 10ft across, with tentacles up to 65ft long.

Color: very varied, from transparent to dull to brilliant.

Species mentioned in text:
Beadlet anemone (*Actinia equina*)
Blue cyanea jellyfish (*Cyanea lamarcki*)
Common jellyfish (*Aurelia aurita*)
Compass jellyfish (*Chrysaora hyoscella*)
Hydra (e.g., *Hydra viridissima*)
Portuguese man-o'-war (*Physalia physalis*)

Most of the animals of the jellyfish and anemone group (Cnidaria) live in the sea, but a few species are found in fresh water, including the small anemone-like *Hydra*, which is very common in canals, ponds and lakes.

SIMPLE, BUT COMPLICATED
Although the cnidarian body plan is a simple one, there are many variations in the animals' shapes, and also in their life histories. Some kinds have a jellyfish stage that reproduces sexually, giving a larva that settles on the seabed to become a polyp. The polyp reproduces asexually, dividing to form little jellyfish. These break off and swim away to an independent life, and start the cycle again.

In large species of jellyfish, the polyp stage lasts only a short while. In sea anemones, the jellyfish stage has disappeared. They can reproduce sexually, or by budding.

LIVING TOGETHER
Many polyps live together in colonies. Their mouths and tentacles are separate, but their bodies are joined by strips of tissue at the base. Colonies may be tiny, like those of some of the sea firs to be found on the shore. Or they can be very large, especially in those cnidarians known as corals (see pages 20-23).

Confusingly, some of the animals that at first sight seem to be jellyfish turn out, when examined closely, to

◄Sea anemones rest attached to the seabed waiting for food. They are often well camouflaged against being found by large prey.

▲ Red, strawberry or green (as here) colored, the Beadlet anemone, 3in tall, is common on European coasts.

▼ The Compass jellyfish can have a bell 12in across. It has 24 stinging tentacles, and 4 long mouth "arms."

be colonies of polyps. An example is the Portuguese man-o'-war. It has an air-filled jelly float on the surface that allows it to be carried by the wind. Below this are many polyps. Some are tentacle-like and sting for food and defense. Others act as mouths for the colony. Several polyps are specialized for reproduction.

STINGS

A special characteristic of animals of the jellyfish and sea anemone group are the arrays of stinging cells on their tentacles. Inside each cell is a barbed thread coiled up. When prey or an enemy touches the tentacle, it triggers the cells to fire out their threads. This punctures and holds the prey, and injects venom.

Other cells on the tentacles shoot out threads which entangle prey. A person touching the tentacles of small anemones on the shore can feel these threads grip. Some species of jellyfish and anemone can capture and paralyze large fish. Many species, though, feed on small particles of food in the water, which they capture on sticky mucus on the tentacles.

SWIMMING AND DRIFTING

Many jellyfish are active swimmers. Repeatedly, they relax muscles in the bell, then contract them, shooting out bursts of water for a kind of jet propulsion. But often the jellyfish is not strong enough to swim against the currents in the ocean's surface, and gets carried along by them.

To help keep their muscles moving together, jellyfish have a ring of nerves around the bell. They also have simple sense organs. The Common jellyfish has eight notches round its rim. In each is a pigment spot that is very sensitive to light. There is also a small hard pellet in a special body cavity. As the bell tips, the pellet presses against the top or bottom of the cavity. Using this information the jellyfish can keep on an even keel.

Most jellyfish are only a few inches across, but some species can grow very large. The Blue cyanea is generally about 8in in diameter, but some individuals have been seen more than 10ft across, trailing tentacles many yards long. A large Portuguese man-o'-war may have tentacles over 60ft long trailing behind. Although they are simple animals such giants are among the biggest of the animals without backbones (invertebrates). Also, the stings of both these species can be dangerous to humans.

STANDING AND WAITING

Sea anemones are usually fixed to the seabed and play a waiting game. They wait for small animals to blunder into their tentacles or to be carried there by water currents. Then they trap them and the tentacles fold over to push the victims into the mouth.

Many kinds of anemone live on the shore. If they are uncovered by the tide, they fold in their tentacles and become rounded blobs. Once covered by water again, they emerge, spreading their tentacles wide to give the maximum chance of catching food. Other kinds live deeper in the sea, stretching wide to catch food falling from above. Some burrowing anemones live in sand with only the tentacles around the mouth exposed.

NEIGHBORLY FIGHTS

Although sea anemones usually stay in one place, some of them can move about slowly. They may glide on their bases. Some even move by somersaulting. Beadlet anemones have even been seen to fight one another, one bending over slowly – this may take 10 minutes – to give a sting to the other. Usually the biggest wins. Such fights may help clear a good feeding space for an anemone.

◀▼ Mediterranean and North Atlantic sea anemones and jellyfish The 8in-across *Cyanea lamarcki* (1) has a powerful sting. Common jellyfish (2), up to 10in across. Portuguese man-o'-war (3), extends to 12in long. Beadlet anemone (4). Plumose anemone (*Metridium senile*) (5), to 3in or more. *Obelia geniculata* (6), a colony, up to 1½in tall. *Sertularia operculata* (7), a colony, to 18in high. *Eunicella verrucosa* (8), a sea fan, colony to 12in high. *Peachia hastata* (9), a burrowing anemone 4in long. Jewel anemone (*Corynactis viridis*) (10), about ⅕in across. Dead man's fingers (*Alcyonium digitatum*) (11), colony height 8in.

CORALS

From an orbiting space station, the astronauts look down at the Earth. As they pass over Australia they see a line running down the east coast where the sea is a different color. They are looking at a structure 1,200mi long, the biggest ever built by living creatures. It is the Great Barrier Reef, built by millions of coral polyps over millions of years.

Corals are colonies of sea anemone-like creatures (see pages 16-19), to which they are related. The polyps make skeletons of some kind and are given the name coral, but the type that build huge reefs are those known as stony corals. These are found only in areas of sea close to the shore in the tropics where the water is clear, as mud and silt can soon bury and kill corals. There are corals in cooler climates. For example, there are many solitary corals living off European coasts. But the greatest abundance and development of coral is in warm seas.

DEPENDENT ON LODGERS
Reef-building corals are dependent on single-celled algae that live inside them. The algae make food by using sunlight, so they must be near enough

to the surface for light to reach them. In especially clear water, this may be possible to depths of 250ft. They also need a temperature of 70°F to do well. The algae help get the lime out of seawater that the corals use for their skeletons and provide some oxygen.

SKELETONS
The skeleton of a coral polyp is secreted by the animal's base. When a polyp separates (buds off) from its parent, the two organisms remain connected to one another by strips of

▲ Dead corals provide a support for other organisms. Here polyps grow on the dead skeleton of a coral colony.

▶ A coral reef in the Red Sea containing many different species. The reef is home to fish and other animals.

tissue that extend sideways. As new polyps secrete skeleton around their bases, so the lime builds up more and more. The living polyps may form a skin on an enormous block of coral that is full of holes, the little sockets marking where their ancestors lived.

Different species of coral bud and grow in different patterns. There are brain corals and staghorn corals, their names reflecting the shapes they grow into. Sometimes one area of reef will be made up of a single type of coral. More often corals of all shapes and sizes will be growing together.

DAY AND NIGHT
Some corals are active most of the time, but during the day on a coral reef it is often just the hard, rough coral skeletons that are readily visible. Their owners are withdrawn into their sockets. By night, the reef looks very different. The millions of tiny polyps

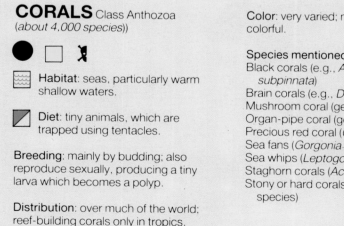

CORALS Class Anthozoa
(*about 4,000 species*))

● □ ✗

Habitat: seas, particularly warm shallow waters.

Diet: tiny animals, which are trapped using tentacles.

Breeding: mainly by budding; also reproduce sexually, producing a tiny larva which becomes a polyp.

Distribution: over much of the world; reef-building corals only in tropics.

Color: very varied; many extremely colorful.

Species mentioned in text:
Black corals (e.g., *Antipathes subpinnata*)
Brain corals (e.g., *Diploria strigosa*)
Mushroom coral (genus *Fungia*)
Organ-pipe coral (genus *Tubipora*)
Precious red coral (*Corallium rubrum*)
Sea fans (*Gorgonia* species)
Sea whips (*Leptogorgia* species)
Staghorn corals (*Acropora* species)
Stony or hard corals (e.g., *Madrepora* species)

emerge to clothe the skeletons in soft bodies and waving tentacles, giving an altogether softer outline to the reef. Small planktonic animals come nearer to the sea's surface in the darkness to feed on planktonic plants. The polyps catch them with their tentacles, bring them to the mouth, then eat them.

OTHER FORMS AND LIFE-STYLES
The black corals are a group that do not build reefs. Instead they form slender plant-like colonies with a horny skeleton. The polyps surround this and cannot be retracted. The skeleton has many thorns.

The gorgonians, or horny corals, make branching colonies looking a little like trees. They are called sea fans and sea whips. Because their skeleton is horny they sway in the sea currents. Some of them are brilliantly colored. Precious red coral, used in jewelry, belongs to this group. It has become rare in many places as a result of being collected by people in too great a number. This coral strengthens its body with lime particles. In the middle of the colony these fuse into a hard block. It is this which is cut out and shaped for ornament.

The Organ-pipe coral of tropical waters has yet another growth form, with the polyps in vertical tubes connected by evenly spaced horizontal cross-bars. The stony skeleton of the mushroom corals looks like the gills of a huge upturned mushroom.

▲ This coral has used its stinging cells to paralyze a worm. Between the main polyps are smaller budded polyps.

KINDS OF REEF
In 1842 the English biologist Charles Darwin noticed that there are three main ways in which reefs grow. Some form close to the shore on rocky coastlines. These are called fringing reefs. Others are separated from the shore by lagoons or channels. They are known as barrier reefs. They have formed as the seabed subsided.

The third sort of reef is the atoll, a circle of coral, with or without an island in the middle. An atoll forms where an undersea volcano pushes out from the water to form an island,

and then slowly sinks. A coral reef forms on its fringes, growing upwards to keep pace with the sinking land. In some places coral reefs have been growing upward at the rate of about $^{1}/_{2}$in a year for thousands of years.

EVERYTHING IN ITS PLACE

Different parts of a coral reef are home to different species. On the side of the reef exposed to wind and waves, the reef-building corals and seaweeds grow well. Lower down in the water, below 160ft, these do not grow so well. There, conditions suit solitary corals and the waving sea fans.

The crests of reefs suit yet other species, such as the staghorn corals, which provide shelter for many small fish. Some corals grow happily over a range of depths, but others change their skeleton shape according to the conditions – lumpy if they live near the surface, delicately branched if they are at depth. In some shallow-water forms, the polyps are open most of the time, but the same species may open only at night in deeper water.

LARVAL SEARCH

Although most corals reproduce by budding, the polyps may sometimes reproduce sexually. The result is a tiny flattened swimming larva. This searches for a well-lit empty patch of reef on which to settle. Many never find a suitable site and die. Those that do, change into polyps. Only a few of these thrive, but those that succeed will split many times to produce the typical reef-building coral with its millions of polyps and huge skeleton.

▲ ▼ In some corals, such as the brain corals, a new polyp may not completely separate from its parent. This results in a group of joined polyps, separated from others by a ridge. Such a group can be seen above. The result is the ridged mound (brain-shaped) skeleton below.

WORMS

A tiny worm burrows from inside a blood vessel into the air tubes in a child's lung. It climbs upwards to the throat, and is swallowed with food down into the intestine. Here it stays, growing fast on the digested food, until it is 12in long. It is a roundworm, one of many kinds that are parasites of people.

What is a worm? There is in fact no scientific definition of a worm. The name is given to many creatures that are long and thin, and have a front (head) end and a back (tail) end. But this type of body has evolved many times among the animals. Numerous quite unrelated species of animal are all called worms.

The best known group of worms is the annelids, or segmented worms. These are dealt with elsewhere and include the earthworms (pages 28-29), the ragworms (pages 30-33) and the leeches (pages 34-35). Another distinctive group are the flatworms (pages 26-27). In addition to all these there are some ten major types of animal that have worm-like bodies.

IN THE SEA

Several worm types, such as priapulans and sipunculans, live only in the sea. They are bottom-dwellers, feeding on tiny particles of food either filtered from the water or sifted from mud. Acorn worms are another kind of filter-feeder, but they use their gills not their mouths as sieves.

One of the oddest worm groups are the beard worms. They have bodies up to 60in in length, but they are never wider than about 1/8in. They live in tubes on the seabed. They have no gut (digestive tube). They seem to absorb molecules of food through their skin or perhaps through the "beard," which consists of a bunch of tentacles at the front end.

GUTLESS

Yet another group, the spiny-headed worms, also have no gut. They live as

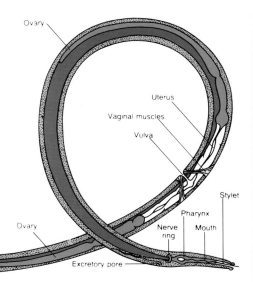

▶Roundworms have a spike-like stylet in front of the mouth that allows them to pierce their food. A thick but flexible skin protects them. In these worms the sexes are separate. This is a female.

parasites in the intestines of such backboned animals as birds and fish.

Horsehair worms live in the soil around ponds and streams, and lay their eggs in water on plants. The larvae are parasites on insects such as crickets and grasshoppers. Development takes several months before the adult worm leaves the host.

ROUNDWORMS

Roundworms are one of the most successful groups of animals, having a wide and varied distribution. But they are not particularly conspicuous. They live in all kinds of water, and in damp soil.

All roundworms look remarkably similar. They are long, with pointed ends, and have a featureless body covered in a tough skin that little can penetrate. This is one reason why many can survive as parasites. These live inside plants and animals, including people. Some are pests of crops, or cause major diseases. In some parts of the world nearly three-quarters of the human population may be infected with some kind of roundworm. *Ascaris lumbricoides* is one of the largest species. It lives in the human gut. Similar roundworms live in pigs and many other mammals.

WORMS (*12 phyla including about 30,600 species*)

⬭ ▭

〰️ **Habitat:** fresh water, seas, damp soil; many are parasites.

◪ **Diet:** varied; feed on animals, plants, decomposing organic matter, or as parasites.

Breeding: sexes separate or combined (hermaphrodite); tiny eggs may have tough shell and up to 200,000 a day laid by some parasites. Larvae may live in different habitat from adults (roundworms).

Distribution: worldwide.

Size: from microscopic to 50in long but most about 1/20in in length.

Color: mostly dull or colorless.

Species mentioned in text:
Ascaris lumbricoides (Intestinal roundworm)
Acorn worms Phylum Hemichordata (90 species)
Beard worms Phylum Pogonophora (150 species)
Echiurans Phylum Echiura (130 species)
Horsehair worms Phylum Nematomorpha (80 species)
Priapulans Phylum Priapula (9 species)
Roundworms Phylum Nematoda (12,000 species)
Sipunculans Phylum Sipuncula (320 species)
Spiny-headed worms Phylum Acanthocephala (700 species)

▼**North Atlantic marine worm species**
Echiurans such as the 3in-long *Thalassema neptuni* (1) live in soft mud or in holes in rock. They are found down to 33,000ft and catch food particles on sticky mucus on the front. Priapulans, for example *Priapulus caudatus* (2), live in soft mud on the sea bottom. The front of the head end can be turned inside out to catch prey, and is armed with many teeth. *Chaetopterus variopedatus* (3) is a ragworm (see pages 30-33). *Phascolion strombi* (4) is a sipunculan that makes a mud burrow in empty shells.

▲Massed horsehair worms under a stone in a drying stream bed. These worms are often found in horses' drinking troughs. For this reason the myth grew up that they were horsehairs come to life.

FLATWORMS

A sheep lowers its head to crop the lush grass. But there is a hidden danger. Minute resting-stage larvae of a parasite are on the grass. Eaten by the sheep, these migrate to the liver, where they feed and grow into adult Liver flukes. This sheep is lucky as only a few flukes develop. Its neighbor, infested with dozens, dies after a few weeks.

Two-thirds of all flatworms are parasites, feeding on the tissues of other animals, their hosts, while living on or inside them. There are two main types, the flukes and the tapeworms. All other flatworms are free-living.

GUT INVADERS

Tapeworms are long and ribbon-like. They have no mouth or digestive system. They live in the intestines of other animals, bathed in food which they absorb through their skin.

On its head, a tapeworm has hooks which it uses to anchor itself to the host's gut wall. Behind the head, the body grows section by section to form a chain. Although nerves extend from the head to the rear of the worm, the sections are almost independent of one another. When fully developed, they are little more than bags of reproductive organs. A ripe section full of eggs detaches itself and passes out of the host with the feces.

HUMAN PARASITES

The Beef and Pork tapeworms live as adults in people. After their eggs pass out in human feces, they may contaminate grass. If a cow or pig eats this, the shell of each egg is digested. The released embryo bores through the gut wall and is carried via the blood to a muscle. It turns into a little bladder-shaped resting stage. If a person poorly cooks infested meat, this stage may not be killed and the hooked head of the adult worm is released and fastens to the gut wall.

One of the most dangerous tapeworms to humans is the Dog tapeworm. It is tiny as an adult in the dog, but larval stages can live in people. Eggs can be transferred to a person from a dog's tongue. The cyst (resting stage) can be bigger than an orange. If a cyst forms in the brain, it can be fatal.

FREE-LIVING FLATWORMS

Planarians are free-living flatworms of fresh and sea water. Some live in such damp places as rain forests. They feed on protozoans, small crustaceans, snails and other worms by pushing out through the mouth a muscular tube, the pharynx, which tears flesh and vacuums it up.

FLATWORMS Phylum Platyhelminthes (5,600 species)

Habitat: majority parasitic; others live in water and damp places.

Diet: eat whole small animals, or feed on the tissues, digested food or body fluids of animals large and small.

Breeding: individuals usually both male and female (hermaphrodite). Larval stages often very different to adult in shape and habitat. In parasitic forms may be several larval stages which parasitise a different host from the adult.

Distribution: worldwide; harmful human parasites mainly in tropics and sub-tropics.

Size: microscopic to 13ft in length, but most $1/200$-$1/6$in long.

Color: mostly white, black, gray, or flesh-colored. Some brightly colored or patterned.

Species mentioned in text:
Banded planarian (*Prostheceraeus vittatus*)
Beef tapeworm (*Taenia saginata*)
Dog tapeworm (*Echinococcus granulosus*)
Liver fluke (*Fasciola hepatica*)
Pork tapeworm (*Taenia solium*)

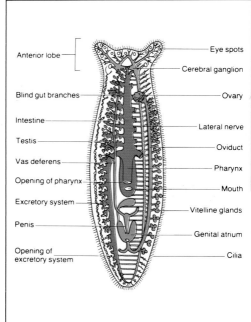

Anterior lobe — Eye spots
— Cerebral ganglion
Blind gut branches — Ovary
Intestine — Lateral nerve
Testis — Oviduct
Vas deferens — Pharynx
Opening of pharynx — Mouth
Excretory system — Vitelline glands
Penis — Genital atrium
Opening of excretory system — Cilia

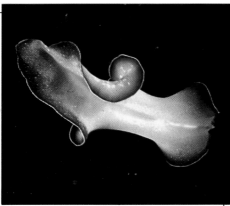

▲ The aquatic *Pseudoceros* shows the thin body typical of flatworms.

◄ Diagram of the planarian flatworm body plan. The mouth and pharynx are halfway down the body. The gut is branched "blind" (lacks an anus). The animal is both male and female.

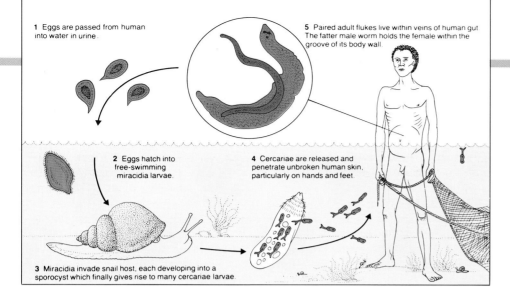

1 Eggs are passed from human into water in urine.

5 Paired adult flukes live within veins of human gut. The fatter male worm holds the female within the groove of its body wall.

2 Eggs hatch into free-swimming miracidia larvae.

4 Cercariae are released and penetrate unbroken human skin, particularly on hands and feet.

3 Miracidia invade snail host, each developing into a sporocyst which finally gives rise to many cercariae larvae.

▲ Life cycle of the human blood fluke *Schistosoma haematobium*. It damages the person's bladder wall as its eggs bore through. This parasite lives in Africa and the Middle East and infects several million people.

▼ A Banded planarian slides smoothly through a bed of sea squirts. Most free-living flatworms such as this colorful marine species avoid strong light and hide under stones and among vegetation most of the time.

Planarians are good at regenerating parts of their bodies. Many can grow a whole new body from just a tiny fragment. Some planarians reproduce asexually when they get to a certain length. The head "loses control" over the rear part of the body, which then splits off and becomes a complete new animal.

Most free-living flatworms are small and live in fresh water, gliding around on the carpet of tiny hairs (cilia) that covers their bodies. Their marine relatives are usually very thin and leaf-like, and may be very brightly colored. One small marine flatworm, *Convoluta*, is green because it has tiny algae living in it. These produce all the food the adult worm needs.

EARTHWORMS

An earthworm emerges from its burrow in the early morning. It has spent part of the night gathering leaves. There are still some within reach, but now the worm feels sunlight on its back, and it hesitates. This saves its life. A sharp-sighted blackbird has seen it, and makes a grab at the head. But enough of the worm is still below ground to get a good grip on the burrow sides. It tugs itself back in and pulls its slimy head from the bird's grasp. This time, the early bird has failed to catch the worm.

Earthworms are segmented worms, also called annelids. Other annelids include the ragworms (pages 30-33) and the leeches (pages 34-35). Only these worms have bodies with many distinct and basically similar segments running all the way from head to tail. Individuals may have more than 200 segments.

Ordinary earthworms are burrowing animals, and they are found all round the world in all kinds of soil. But this order of animals also contains freshwater species, such as the bloodworms that live in river and lake mud, and some marine species. Many earthworms are pink because they have a red oxygen-carrying hemoglobin pigment like ours in their blood. Even in stagnant water, bloodworms are able to extract enough oxygen to live using their hemoglobin.

SEETHING SOIL

In some soils, earthworms may live in very large numbers. In old meadow soil in Europe there can be more than 700 Common earthworms beneath each square yard of ground. Several kinds of earthworm produce coiled masses, or "casts," of soil that has passed through their digestive system. This continually brings fertile soil to the surface. The biologist Charles Darwin observed worms in action, and calculated that together they might deposit 10 tons of soil on each acre of surface in a year. This may be an underestimate in some places. The action of worms also aerates the soil and can improve the drainage.

Most worms eat dead fragments of plants. Decaying roots and leaves are consumed, and soil is taken in and any edible fragments digested. The

◄An earthworm is both male and female, but a pair come together to mate in a slimy embrace. Each passes sperm to the other.

▼A diagram of an earthworm, cut away to show some of the organs inside. Many of the rear segments are rather similar to each other, but the hearts, brain and reproductive organs are towards the front of the worm. The mouth is under the lip (prostomium).

EARTHWORMS Class Clitellata, Order Oligochaeta (*3,000 species*)

Habitat: soil, except where frozen or too acid; also some in fresh water and on seashore.

Diet: many extract fragments of plant material from soil and mud.

Breeding: each animal is both male and female; lay eggs which hatch as small worms. Asexual reproduction in some species.

Distribution: worldwide.

Size: length 1/20in to 10ft, but most species up to about 12in.

Color: pink, red, some brownish or greenish.

Species mentioned in text:
Australian giant worm
   (*Megascolecides* species)
Brandling (*Eisenia fetida*)
Common European earthworm
   (*Lumbricus terrestris*)
South African giant worm
   (*Microchaetus rappi*)

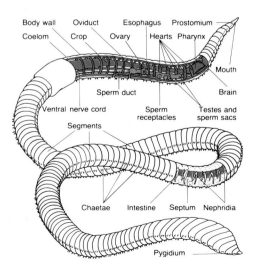

Body wall — Oviduct — Esophagus — Prostomium
Coelom — Crop — Ovary — Hearts — Pharynx
Mouth
Brain
Sperm duct
Ventral nerve cord — Sperm receptacles — Testes and sperm sacs
Segments
Chaetae — Intestine — Septum — Nephridia
Pygidium

brandling is a small worm living in the leaf litter in woodlands. It is good at breaking down garden compost too.

EXTENDABLE GIANTS

Ordinary earthworms are up to 12in long. Many are smaller. But in several parts of the world there are giants. In North America, giant worms live in Oregon and Washington, and one Australian species grows to 10ft or more in length. South African giant earthworms regularly reach 5ft, and one is on record at 11ft. This was its resting length. When fully stretched out and moving it was nearly twice as long. Unfortunately, several of these giants may be threatened animals as a result of destruction of their habitats.

WORM'S EYE VIEW

An earthworm does not have eyes like ours, but it does have cells that are sensitive to light. These may even have small lenses on their surface. The sensitive cells are along the back of the worm, and especially at the extreme front, on the overhanging lip called the prostomium. There are also sense

▲ ► Some worms feed on rotting leaves. They come to the surface at night and pull the leaves by their narrowest ends into the burrow entrance.

cells that can detect chemical stimuli, again, mostly concentrated on the prostomium. Touch cells are found all over the skin, with up to 1,000 on a single segment. Each of these has a microscopic hair sticking out.

Rather larger hairs, called chaetae, are also found in the skin. The earthworms' Order name, Oligochaeta, means few bristles. Ordinary earthworms have just eight bristles on each segment. They can be moved in and out. The worm uses them to grip the ground or the inside of its burrow.

FROM EGG TO ADULT

After mating, earthworms lay several eggs in a cocoon. Often only one egg survives to hatch. The cocoon is secreted by the thickened "saddle," which can be seen about a third of the way down each worm. The eggs hatch as tiny worms, which may take a year to become adult. Some species can live 10 years if they get the chance.

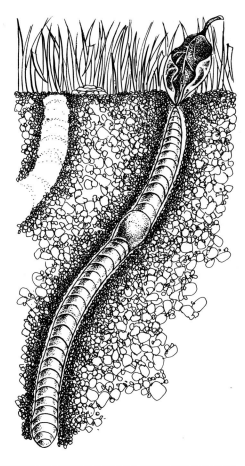

RAGWORMS

It is a few days after the full Moon. A greenish glow fills the surface water of the sea off the Pacific island of Fiji. It is caused by dozens of glowing female Palolo worms. Now flashes of light show where male Palolo worms are swimming towards them. A male and female come close. They writhe about for several minutes then burst, emptying sperm and eggs into the sea. The adults die almost immediately. The tiny fertilized eggs soon develop into larvae.

RAGWORMS Class
Polychaeta (8,000 species)

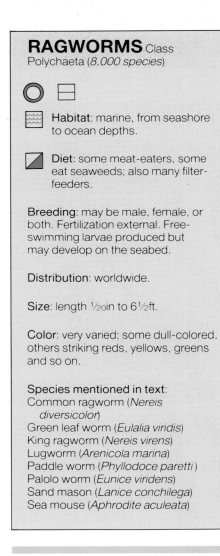

Habitat: marine, from seashore to ocean depths.

Diet: some meat-eaters, some eat seaweeds; also many filter-feeders.

Breeding: may be male, female, or both. Fertilization external. Free-swimming larvae produced but may develop on the seabed.

Distribution: worldwide.

Size: length ¹⁄₂₀in to 6½ft.

Color: very varied; some dull-colored, others striking reds, yellows, greens and so on.

Species mentioned in text:
Common ragworm (*Nereis diversicolor*)
Green leaf worm (*Eulalia viridis*)
King ragworm (*Nereis virens*)
Lugworm (*Arenicola marina*)
Paddle worm (*Phyllodoce paretti*)
Palolo worm (*Eunice viridens*)
Sand mason (*Lanice conchilega*)
Sea mouse (*Aphrodite aculeata*)

The ragworms and their relations, collectively known as the polychaete worms, are very numerous and varied – so varied that they are divided into some 80 families. All of them are sea animals. They are found from the tidal parts of the shore to the depths of the ocean. Some crawl and walk across the seabed. Many are free-swimming or live in the plankton. Several species are parasites. Others live on the seabed in permanent burrows or tubes they make themselves.

PADDLING ALONG
Polychaete worms are made up of a series of body units or segments. Each has a pair of two-lobed extensions called parapodia. Each of these has a pair of sensory tentacles and two bundles of stiff hairs, or chaetae. (Polychaete means many chaetae.) The parapodia function as legs when crawling, and as paddles when swimming. They are best developed in active worms that crawl on the seabed or swim well. The Paddle worm of European shores, which both swims and crawls, has some 200 segments, each with a pair of leaf-like parapodia.

PREDATORS AND BROWSERS
The Common ragworm of the middle and lower shores of Europe spends most of its time in a burrow in the sand, popping up its head now and then. It can, however, swim and crawl well. It grows to 5in in length, and is

▲A fine felt of silky hair-like chaetae gives the Sea mouse its furry appearance. The back chaetae are brown, those on its sides shiny.

a fierce predator. It seizes small soft-bodied animals, fish eggs and larvae by pushing out its pharynx (throat) from inside its mouth and grabbing with its strong horny jaws. The King ragworm has similar habits, but can grow to 16in long. Some of the large ragworms can give a very painful bite to humans. These species have many sense organs at the head end to help them find their food – four eyes, two antennae, and four pairs of tentacles.

Several kinds of ragworm eat both animal and plant material, and a few feed just on seaweeds. Ragworms come in many colors, from red and brown to bluish or even green. The Green leaf worm lives in crevices in rocks, and when the tide is out may wander over the rocks. It is bright green. Even its egg cases are green.

ALL CHANGE TO BREED
When their breeding time arrives, ragworms change their form and habits. The rear segments of their bodies develop specially large parapodia for swimming and produce many sex cells. Each worm leaves its burrow to swim close to the surface in search of the opposite sex. When they meet, sperm and eggs are shed into the sea. The adults then die.

In many ragworms there is a very definite breeding season. One of the most precisely timed of these is that of the Palolo worm of the South Pacific, in which mating takes place at dawn one week after the November full Moon. In this species the front of the worm stays hidden in a burrow in a crevice among the rocks on a reef. The rear part develops sex cells – sperm or eggs, not both – and changes shape and color – the male's is colored reddish-brown and the female's blue-green by the sex cells within. On the appointed day, the rear part breaks off and swims to the surface. Here it joins countless others in a writhing mass, shedding its sex cells then dying. The front part of the worm, left behind, grows a new tail. A year later this may take part in the mating swarm.

AN ATYPICAL WORM

The polychaete *Tomopteris* is a small worm that permanently swims in the plankton of the sea's surface. It is transparent and almost colorless. Its parapodia lack chaetae, but are well developed for swimming, and they possess light-producing organs. The head is hammer-shaped, has prominent eyes, and bears two tentacles that are each about two-thirds the length of the body.

BURROWERS

Ragworms that spend their lives in a burrow on the seabed do not need large parapodia for movement. Nor do they need such elaborate sense organs as some of the predatory species. Types like the lugworm resemble earthworms, but they have many chaetae and each segment at the middle of the body has a pair of small frilly gills. These worms keep a flow of water through their U-shaped burrows that brings them oxygen and allows them to sense signs of food nearby. They have a pharynx, which can be turned out to help gather food particles in the water.

▲Two fanworms, species *Protula maximus*, use their very gaily colored crowns as feeding organs and gills. The rest of the bodies of the worms remain constantly in their tubes.

▼The tubeworm *Serpula vermicularis* spends its adult life in its chalky tube. A pair of feathery gills extracts food and oxygen from water. Between them is the stopper that can plug the tube.

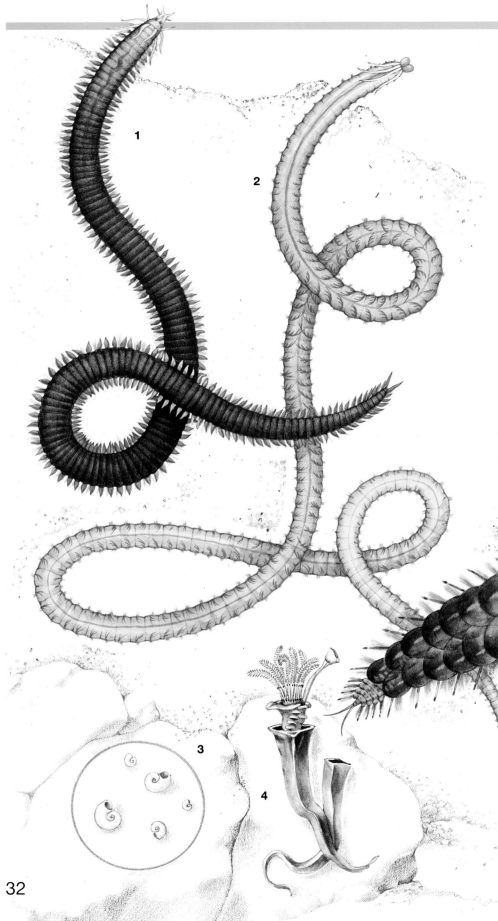

The lugworm eats sand and mud, uses the food within, then pushes out the waste on the sand's surface. When the tide is out, lugworm casts may be seen. Like their land-living counterparts, these worms turn over tons of mud in a year. Lugworms are often dug up by people for fishing bait, and their casts give their presence away. In various parts of the world, many other sand-living polychaetes are used for the same purpose.

FLASHY WORMS

Scaleworms live mainly on the shore. Their backs are covered in scales that overlap and provide excellent camouflage. Some species have the ability to make their scales flash with light if they are alarmed.

One particularly large and specialized scaleworm is the Sea mouse. Up to 8in long, it inhabits sandy bottoms below the tide level. It lives just under the surface of the sand and is usually slow-moving, but it can scuttle a short distance if disturbed.

FANS AND TUBES

Many polychaetes live all the time in tubes. These may be hard and limy, like the tiny curled tubes of *Spirorbis* found on weeds and rocks or the triangular tubes of *Pomatoceros*. They may be of sand or pieces of shell stuck together with a slimy secretion, as in the Sand mason. Usually the worms' parapodia are reduced, and most of the body is of simple structure. The head, though, is often crowned with a ring or fan of delicate and colorful cilia-covered tentacles.

These tentacles perform a dual purpose. They act as gills for breathing and as feeding organs. Fanworms trap minute animals and plants and scraps of food in the water on the tentacles, and the rows of cilia kick these food particles down to the mouth.

The tubes of fanworms give them some protection from predators, but the spreading tentacles are vulnerable. If alarmed, fanworms retract their tentacles and head very suddenly into their tubes.

◀▼**Species of seabed polychaete worms** From the North Atlantic: *Eulalia viridis* (1). *Marphysa sanguinea* (2). Tubeworms *Spirorbis borealis* (3) and *Pomatoceros triqueter* (4). Scaleworm *Harmothoe imbricata* (5). From the Mediterranean: *Hermodice carunculata* (6). *Perinereis nuntia* (7). From the Indo-Pacific: tentacles of *Reteterebella queenslandica* (8). *Sabellastarte intica* (9). *Spirobranchus gigantens* (10).

LEECHES

A group of people push their way through an Asian forest. It is the rainy season and the trees and ground vegetation are dripping wet. Unnoticed by the walkers, as they brush past the plants some animals fasten themselves to their skin. They are leeches, preparing to suck a meal of blood from their victims.

Leeches are segmented worms with few outside features except for the suckers at each end. The large circular hind sucker is usually easy to see. The smaller front sucker around the mouth may be clearly visible, as in fish leeches, or it may be hard to see.

Most leeches have no bristles, or chaetae, on their skin, and unlike other segmented worms (see pages 28-33) they have a fixed number (33) of segments. Like earthworms, they have a saddle (clitellum) which makes the egg cocoon.

Leech skin is quite thin and slimy. Leeches live mainly in fresh water, but a few are sea animals. Some live on land in very damp habitats such as rain forests. Leeches change their shape as they move about, and may become much fatter after a good meal.

SUCKING AND BITING
Some kinds of leech eat other invertebrates (animals without a backbone) and swallow them whole. European leeches of the genus *Tracheta* live partly on land, and may be found in drains and wastepipes. Up to 4in in length, they feed on slugs and earthworms. Other leeches suck the body fluids of invertebrates. But many species are adapted for feeding on the blood of vertebrates, including humans.

A MEDICAL AID
The Medicinal leech gets its name, not from being swallowed as medicine, but because it has been used for centuries for bloodletting by doctors and others. At one time, bleeding a patient was considered good for all sorts of illnesses. The Medicinal leech was ideal for the job, as it likes to feed on large mammals such as humans, as well as on amphibians and fish.

Once attached to a victim, the Medicinal leech cuts into their skin with its jaws, then draws out blood by a pumping action. At the same time, the leech secretes chemicals into the victim. These distend the blood vessels, make the blood run rather than clot, and act as an anesthetic.

A feeding Medicinal leech may take up to five times its own body weight in blood. It soon gets rid of the water content, leaving solids in the pouches of the digestive system. Digestion of such a massive meal may take up to 30 weeks, so the Medicinal leech, like several of the other blood-sucking species, may only need to feed once or twice a year.

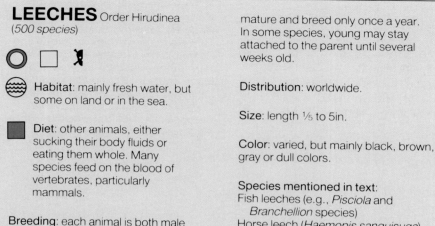

LEECHES Order Hirudinea
(500 species)

Habitat: mainly fresh water, but some on land or in the sea.

Diet: other animals, either sucking their body fluids or eating them whole. Many species feed on the blood of vertebrates, particularly mammals.

Breeding: each animal is both male and female; there is no larval stage. Most species take a year or more to mature and breed only once a year. In some species, young may stay attached to the parent until several weeks old.

Distribution: worldwide.

Size: length ⅕ to 5in.

Color: varied, but mainly black, brown, gray or dull colors.

Species mentioned in text:
Fish leeches (e.g., *Pisciola* and *Branchellion* species)
Horse leech (*Haemopis sanguisuga*)
Medicinal leech (*Hirudo medicinalis*)

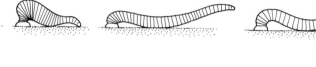

▼The internal structure of a leech. The gut is shown purple, the reproductive organs orange. There is a single pair of ovaries and a series of pairs of testes.

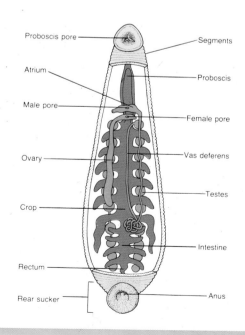

Proboscis pore — Segments
Atrium — Proboscis
Male pore — Female pore
Ovary — Vas deferens
Crop — Testes
Rectum — Intestine
Rear sucker — Anus

▲ A Medicinal leech draws human blood. The rear sucker (behind) can be seen gripping, while the three jaws within the head at the front fasten into the skin making a Y-shaped cut.

► A jawed leech in the north Australian rain forest waits in the leaf litter to pounce upon passing prey.

▼ A leech loops its body as it moves across a solid surface, holding with one end while moving the other.

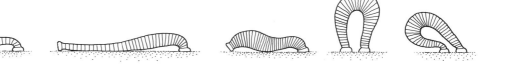

A Medicinal leech is about 3in long at rest. Its relative the Horse leech is only a little smaller, and is more likely to be seen in the wild. In spite of its size and name, it does not feed on horses, having rather weak jaws that cannot even penetrate human skin. Instead it eats invertebrates, sucking their blood, or, if they are small enough, swallowing them whole.

UNDER THREAT

Once common throughout Europe, the Medicinal leech is now found only in a few scattered places. In the past it was collected for bloodletting, and today it is still used in making drugs because of the blood anti-clotting agents in its saliva. But as well as being collected, many of the marshes it liked to live in have been drained.

► *Helobdella stagnalis* is about ½in long at rest. Light shining through it shows its internal organs.

CRUSTACEANS

A scientist looks down a microscope at some water taken from the surface of the sea. A myriad of tiny animals swim into view. These are larvae of types that will settle on the seabed in later life, such as crabs and lobsters. They are species of invertebrates known as crustaceans.

In addition to many familiar animals, such as crabs, the phylum Crustacea includes many smaller relatives, some of which are a major part of the plankton of the sea. The following better-known types of crustacean are dealt with separately: woodlice and their relatives (pages 38-39), barnacles (pages 40-41), shrimps and prawns (pages 42-45), lobsters and crayfish (pages 46-49), hermit crabs (pages 50-53) and crabs (pages 54-57). This article is about crustaceans in general, and some of the lesser known groups.

VARIATIONS ON A BASIC PLAN
Crustaceans have a tough outer skin that acts as their skeleton. They have to shed (molt) this external skeleton periodically in order to grow. Basically, the crustacean body is made of a series of segments, and each segment has a pair of jointed legs. Usually three regions can be seen in the body – the head, thorax and abdomen. The jointed limbs may be adapted for many different jobs. They may be leaf-shaped for swimming, or long walking legs. In some crustaceans parts of the legs are developed as gills. Even the jaws and head appendages, the antennae, are modified legs.

Crustaceans all have two pairs of antennae. Generally they use them as feelers, but some kinds use them for swimming, or even for clasping a mate. The jaws are used to gather or bite food, and are positioned outside and behind the mouth.

CRUSTACEANS Phylum
Crustacea (*39,000 species*)

○ ▭ ⚘

〰 **Habitat:** mainly marine, but some in fresh water and a few on land.

◨ **Diet:** many larger species are meat-eaters, but some eat plants; small species are often filter-feeders.

Breeding: sexes separate; usually produce a larval stage which is often planktonic (floats and drifts freely).

Distribution: worldwide.

Size: range from microscopic ($1/150$in) to 24in or more in length.

Color: varies, from colorless to dull browns and greens, to vivid orange, red and blue.

Species mentioned in text:
Brine shrimps (*Artemia* species)
Fairy shrimps (e.g., *Branchipus* species)
Freshwater copepods (e.g., *Cyclops*)
Marine copepods (e.g., *Calanus* species)
Sea copepods (e.g., *Caligus* species)
Seed-shrimps (e.g., *Cypris* species)
Water fleas (e.g., *Daphnia*)

Inside a crustacean, the organs lie in a blood-filled space. The blood contains the pigment hemocyanin. This carries oxygen, just like hemoglobin in our blood, but is blue not red.

FROM EGG TO ADULT
Crustaceans normally have separate sexes. Once the eggs hatch, the animals pass through a series of larval stages before becoming adults. The first stage is called a nauplius. This has just three pairs of "legs" – two pairs of antennae and a pair of jaws. Often this stage lives in the plankton, so the larvae are dispersed widely and find new homes for their adult life. Depending on the kind of crustacean, a succession of other, increasingly larger, larval stages follow the nauplius. Many of these larvae look very different to the adults.

FLEAS AND FAIRIES
Water fleas are flattened from side to side, with a hard shell (carapace) that encloses the thorax and abdomen, but not the head. Some kinds, such as *Daphnia*, are familiar to fish keepers as fish food. They get their name from the way they "hop" in the water, swimming jerkily by means of strokes

▼Copepod crustaceans are important foods for many other animals in both sea and fresh water. This small planktonic copepod swims well using its two long antennae to row itself along.

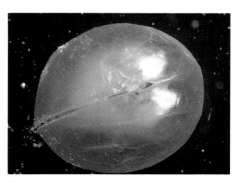

► The rounded two-shelled carapace of this ostracod completely encloses its thorax and abdomen. These tiny crustaceans mostly live on the bottom of aquatic habitats. They use antennae to swim and as feelers.

▼ The freshwater "flea," *Daphnia*, is a type of crustacean. This female bears seven eggs in the brood pouch between her abdomen and carapace.

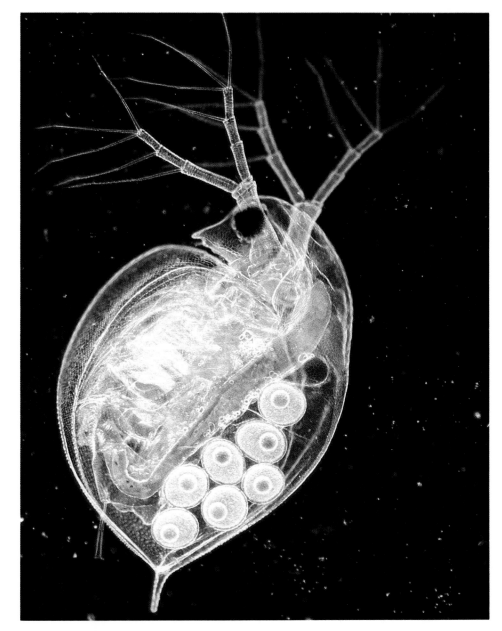

of their antennae. Most live in fresh water and filter out small particles of food using the legs on their thorax.

Water fleas brood their eggs in a special chamber inside the carapace. When the animal next molts, the brood chamber, which now bears fertilized eggs, is cast off. It may withstand drying, freezing, or even passage through the gut of a fish.

Most fairy shrimps live in freshwater pools and springs, where there are no fish to eat them. However, the brine shrimps live in salty lakes. They all have many segments, with feathery limbs that beat in rhythm as they swim, and at the same time filter the water for food. Their eggs are very resistant to drought, so they survive when pools dry up and the adults die. Water fleas and fairy shrimps are all types of branchiopods (820 species).

"HANDLE-FEET" KINDS
Although not familiar to most people, some of the copepod crustaceans (total 8,400 species) that live in sea plankton are among the most abundant animals in the world. More likely to be seen is the copepod *Cyclops*, which inhabits freshwater ponds.

Swimming copepods use a quick jerk of the antennae to escape trouble. They also use their antennae as parachutes to slow their sinking. With their feathery mouthparts they filter food from the water. When tiny plants multiply rapidly in the water, copepods thrive by feeding on them, but they sometimes catch animals too. Copepods are, in turn, prey to fish, molluscs and other aquatic creatures. Some sea copepods are parasites on other animals, including whales.

TOUGHENED SHELL TYPES
Sometimes called seed-shrimps, the ostracods (5,650 species) are small crustaceans with a double shell. They live on the bottom of the sea or of freshwater lakes, feeding on minute plants or fragments of food.

WOODLICE, SANDHOPPERS

A child knocks a piece of bark from a rotten branch. The sudden daylight sends many of the small gray animals beneath it frantically scurrying. They are armor-plated woodlice. Gradually they move away from the bright light and dry air, disappearing once more into damp crevices. Other woodlice each curled into a ball when they were exposed. Soon they, too, unroll and move to a dark, damp place.

◄ Sandhoppers can use their legs to jump and thus escape predators, but they are also good swimmers.

Woodlice are almost the only crustaceans to have made a success of living on land. Some have breathing tubes rather than gills. They brood their young until these hatch, when they look very similar to the adults. But on the whole, woodlice have few special adaptations for living on land. Their skins allow water to be lost from the body fast, and most have to remain in damp places to survive.

PILL BUGS

Some species of woodlouse are called pill bugs because they can roll into a pill-like ball. However, most of them cannot do this, and they always have the flattened shape typical of isopods (meaning those with limbs nearly all alike). Usually seven pairs of walking legs can be seen. Woodlice eat decaying plant matter. Bacteria in their gut help them to digest their food.

Of the many other isopods, most live in the sea, walking on the bottom. Some kinds swim or burrow. The Sea slater, for example, is a large ($\frac{2}{3}$in-long) species that burrows under stones and seaweeds on the shore. The gribble is only $\frac{1}{8}$in long. It is a

pest species because it bores into any wood in the sea with its jaws.

PARASITES AND SCAVENGERS

Isopods such as the hog-louse live in fresh water, crawling over and feeding on dead leaves at the bottom of stagnant water. Some isopods are parasites of fish, hooking themselves on to a host and drawing blood with their jaws. Others are parasites of a type of parasitic barnacle.

Unlike woodlice and their allies, which are all flattened from top to bottom, species of the sandhoppers order, Amphipoda, are flattened from side to side. Often they lie on their sides. The most familiar kinds are the sandhoppers found on sandy shores and the freshwater "shrimp" common in European streams. Most of this order of crustacean are marine, either living on the seabed or swimming close to the surface. They feed by scraping decaying food material from sand grains or filtering plankton with their bristle-covered limbs

Atypical among sandhoppers are a few species that live at the top of the shore on the strand-line. These jump well and also burrow in the sand. Other odd lifestyles among amphipods include swimming and feeding on jellyfish and anemones.

WOODLICE, SANDHOPPERS Orders
Isopoda (*4,000 species*) and Amphipoda (*6,000 species*)

○ □ 🏃

▧ Habitat: sea, fresh water and land.

◩ Diet: most are scavengers, eating pieces of plant and animal; some parasitic species.

Breeding: females hold fertilized eggs in a brood pouch. The eggs hatch as miniature adults.

Distribution: worldwide.

Size: length from $\frac{1}{25}$in (Amphipoda) or $\frac{1}{5}$in (Isopoda) to 1in.

Color: mostly colorless, or dull browns, grays.

Species mentioned in text:
Freshwater "shrimp" (*Gammarus* species)
Gribble (*Limnoria lignorum*)
Hog-louse (*Asellus* species)
Pill bug (*Armadillidium vulgare*)
Sandhopper (*Orchestia* species)
Sea slater (*Ligia oceanica*)

◄The Sea slater lives on the seashore. Its flattened body allows it to shelter in crevices. A male (left in picture) shows seven pairs of legs, a female (right) six pairs.

▼Some species of sandhopper and woodlouse Common European woodlouse (*Oniscus asellus*) (1), often found in gardens. *Gammarus locusta* (2), a sandhopper widespread on beaches, usually beneath seaweed and driftwood. *Talitrus saltator* (3), a sandhopper that lives on the upper shore.

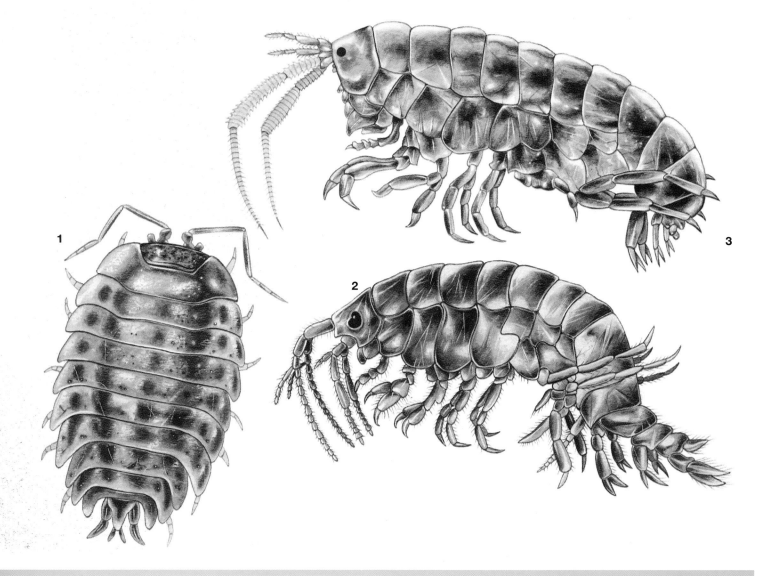

1

2

3

BARNACLES

A giant whale cruises through the water. Hanging from it is a bunch of Goose barnacles. As the whale travels the oceans, it pulls the barnacles through clouds of small animals, which they trap and eat.

Adult barnacles are found attached to solid objects ranging from rocks to living animals such as shellfish, crabs, whales or turtles.

There are three main types of barnacle. Goose barnacles are attached by a stalk to an object. The body at the end of the stalk is covered in hard plates. Acorn barnacles are small cone-shaped shelled animals typically seen attached to rocks on the seashore. At first sight neither of these resembles a crustacean (see pages 36-37). The strong shell plates, made of limy material, are rather like those of a mollusc, such as a snail. Even less like normal crustaceans are the 200 or so species of barnacle that are parasites mainly on crabs. They grow into their host with only their reproductive structures visible on the surface.

FEEDING FEET
When an acorn barnacle is uncovered by the tide it looks lifeless, but when the water covers it, it opens the shell at the top of the cone and its legs emerge. The feathery jointed legs kick food down to the mouth below. These are the equivalent of the legs on the thorax of other crustaceans. Acorn barnacles can filter tiny plants and even bacteria, from the water.

WANDERING LARVAE
At mating time, all neighboring barnacles fertilize one another. The eggs stay within the adult's shell until the larvae hatch. Barnacle larvae are quite different from adults. The first larval stage is a typical crustacean nauplius. It swims in the plankton, filtering tiny plants, for a month or so. Then a different type of larva develops that drifts and swims, but does not feed. Its job is to find a suitable place to settle. Then it attaches itself by the head, and turns into a stationary adult.

▶Hanging Goose barnacles actively feed as they drift through the water. Their limbs rake the water for food.

▼Acorn barnacles live on rocks on the shore. They close up when the tide is out, and can withstand the pounding of heavy waves.

BARNACLES Class
Cirripedia (*1,025 species*)

○ ⊟

Habitat: on rocks, ships and some animals in the sea.

Diet: filter water for small animals and plants.

Breeding: each animal is both male and female; there are swimming and drifting larval stages.

Distribution: worldwide.

Size: microscopic to 30in long.

Color: many have gray or white shells; some brightly colored internally.

Species mentioned in text:
Acorn barnacle (e.g., *Balanus* species)
Goose barnacle (e.g., *Lepas* species)
Parasitic barnacles (e.g., *Sacculina* species)

SHRIMPS, PRAWNS

A prawn walks across the seabed. Much of its body is transparent, but the movement of its limbs and the color of its eyes are seen by a fish. But as the fish moves in to catch the tasty meal, the prawn senses its approach. In a flash, it flicks its tail and shoots backwards to escape.

The terms shrimp and prawn have no exact meaning. Sometimes both are used for the same animal. Shrimps or prawns are simply small members of the order Decapoda, the "ten-legged" crustaceans. These have five pairs of walking legs on the thorax, in addition to limbs modified as mouthparts, swimming organs and so on. The larger decapods are called crabs, lobsters or crayfish (see pages 46-57).

There are about 10,000 species of decapod in over 100 families. About half the families include animals called shrimps or prawns. The shrimp-like krill (order Euphausiacea) are fairly

SHRIMPS, PRAWNS
Orders Decapoda, Stomatopoda, Euphausiacea (*some 5,000 species*)

Habitat: mainly sea and estuary, some on the bottom and some free-swimming; several in fresh water.

Diet: most meat-eating, either large prey or filter-feeding plankton; a few plant-eaters.

Breeding: usually separate sexes; several stages of larvae.

Distribution: worldwide.

Size: length 1/5 to 10in.

Color: varied; colorless, dull browns to vivid reds, yellow, black.

Species mentioned in text:
Banded cleaner shrimp (*Stenopus hispidus*)
Brown shrimp (*Crangon crangon*)
Common prawn (*Leander serratus*)
Krill (e.g., *Euphausia superba*)
Mantis shrimp (e.g., *Squilla mantis*)
Red shrimp (*Pandalus montagui*)
Snapping prawn (e.g., *Alpheus* species)

close relations of the decapods. Less closely related are the mantis shrimps (order Stomatopoda) that are mostly common in tropical seas.

HARD TO SEE
The Brown shrimp of northern temperate seas lives in shallow water and on the lower shore. It is often found where the bottom is sandy, and will go into estuaries. It is about 2in long,

and bears a grayish speckled color which blends well with the background. It can bury itself in sand for protection, and is usually most active at night. Like most bottom-living shrimps, it is a scavenger.

The Common prawn inhabits mostly rocky areas, including pools on the lower shore. It may hide among seaweeds. It is transparent, with small streaks of various colors.

▶Body plan of a prawn. Illustrated is a cutaway of a free-swimming prawn of the genus *Palaemon*. The second walking legs bear pincers. Beneath the abdomen are legs adapted for swimming, called pleopods.

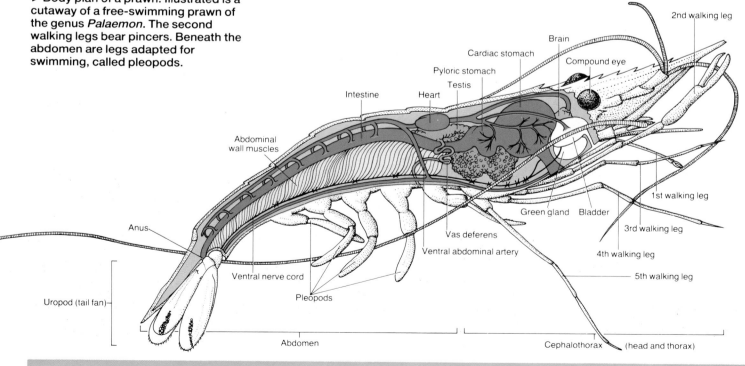

The Common prawn, Brown shrimp and the similar Red shrimp are caught for human consumption around the coasts of Europe and North America.

SNAPPERS AND PUNCHERS

All of the many species of snapping prawn have a special pair of limbs each bearing pincers in which one is usually much better developed. By snapping the large pincers, these prawns can make a loud noise. Not

◄Harvest of the sea: a commercial boat unloads its catch of shrimps at Kachemak Bay in south-west Alaska.

▼Most of this Alaskan catch of shrimps is made up of four species of *Pandalus*. These shrimps are naturally red.

only can this deter an enemy, it can be used to stun prey. Many species are brightly colored, with some of the most spectacular living on coral reefs. Several species of snapping prawn live off European coasts.

Mantis shrimps also pack a punch, sometimes literally so. These heavily armored crustaceans are extremely fierce predators and prey on fish and all types of shellfish. The second thoracic legs are large, but instead of ending in pincers, they have spines and points, or are thickened into "boxing gloves." Like their insect namesake, these shrimps shoot out

◄A Banded cleaner shrimp's colors advertise its services. It cleans fish that have wounds or parasites.

▼An almost transparent anemone shrimp among the tentacles of a sea anemone.

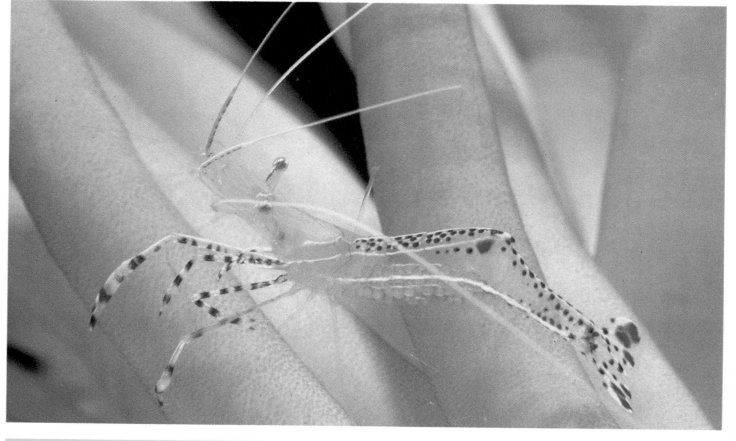

these long legs suddenly to capture prey. They either impale their quarry with a spike, or give such a heavy blow that the prey is stunned or cracked open. Some mantis shrimps grow to 10in long. Each lives in a burrow that it defends against others.

GOING TO THE CLEANERS

Cleaner shrimps feed on parasites of fish. The Banded shrimp is found on reefs in the Pacific and Indian oceans. Rather than just eating the 2in-long shrimp, fish allow it to groom them. These little shrimps often live in pairs.

Several other species of shrimp form associations with other animals. Some small shrimps live on the bodies of sea urchins or starfish, feeding on scraps of food. They are often brilliantly colored to match the body of their associates. On the sea floor, a few species live in partnership with goby fish, a shrimp and a fish sharing the same burrow. The shrimp does most of the excavation and repair work, and may come to the entrance with spoil every minute or so. The goby catches food, which the shrimp shares, and since it has good eyesight, it guards its partner. When it is alarmed, its movements alert the shrimp to danger.

OCEAN SHRIMPS

Many species of shrimp are bottom-dwellers, and swim only occasionally. Others are full-time swimmers, living among the plankton as meat-eaters, feeding on smaller crustaceans and their larvae.

The shrimp-like krill are also swimmers within the plankton. Where conditions are ideal, as in some parts of the southern oceans, they may form shoals with 100 million individuals. Krill have luminous organs, which help them keep in touch with one another. Some of their legs are developed as a filter basket to extract tiny plants from the water. Krill themselves are food for many whales, seals and penguins.

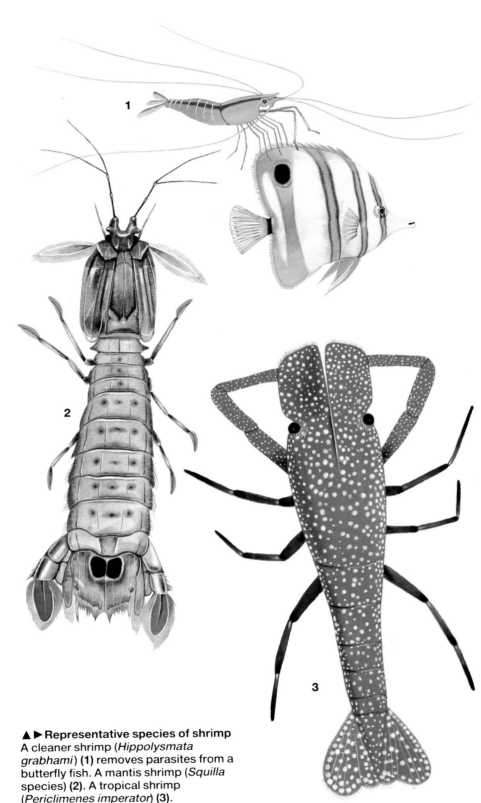

▲ ▶ **Representative species of shrimp**
A cleaner shrimp (*Hippolysmata grabhami*) (1) removes parasites from a butterfly fish. A mantis shrimp (*Squilla* species) (2). A tropical shrimp (*Periclimenes imperator*) (3).

LOBSTERS, CRAYFISH

A lobster pot sits on the seabed, with a bait of pieces of fish inside. From behind a rock the dark shape of a lobster moves towards the pot. But another larger one arrives. The two rivals for the food size up one another. The larger lobster moves towards the other with its huge pincers at the ready. After a brief struggle, the small lobster flees. The large lobster squeezes into the pot and feeds. However, when it tries to leave, it is trapped.

LOBSTERS, CRAYFISH Infraorders
Astacidea, Palinura (*more than 1,500 species*)

○ ⊟ ❌

〜 **Habitat:** seas and fresh water, on the bottom.

▪ **Diet:** mainly meat, often obtained by scavenging, but also hunting prey.

Breeding: sexes separate; female keeps fertilized eggs under her abdomen. Some produce larvae, others young resembling parents.

Distribution: worldwide.

Size: length 4-24in.

Color: very varied; dull browns to bright reds, blues.

Species mentioned in text:
American lobster (*Homarus americanus*)
American spiny lobster (*Panulirus argus*)
European common lobster (*Homarus gammarus*)
European crayfish (*Astacus astacus*)
European spiny lobster (*Palinurus vulgaris*)
Red crayfish (*Astacus fluviatilis*)
Scampi (*Nephrops norvegicus*)

The lobster group includes some of the largest and longest-lived of the crustaceans. Some may live for 100 years or more if they escape the lobster fisherman. The American lobster can be 24in long, and weigh 50lb.

There are two main types of lobster, typical and spiny. Typical lobsters, and crayfish, walk on just four of their five pairs of "walking legs." The front pair have been converted into large pincers, and the next two pairs of legs also have tiny pincers at the end. In the spiny lobsters, also known as rock lobsters and crawfish, there are no pincers. Often the body is very spiny, as the name suggests, and the spines can cause damage to human hands.

Lobsters have long, well-developed abdomens, but the "swimming legs" are too small to propel such large animals, and have other uses.

WEAPONS AND PROTECTION
A large typical lobster, such as the American lobster, can give a powerful nip with its large pincers. It uses them for fighting other lobsters, or for catching and tearing apart prey. The lobsters can catch fish, and break the shells of molluscs to get at the soft parts within. But much of the time, they do not hunt prey and instead feast on the remains of dead animals that fall to the bottom of the sea.

In fact, the pincers on each side are not identical in size and form, except in small lobsters, where they are both thin and toothed. As the lobster goes through successive molts, the pincer on one side becomes larger than the other. Its teeth grow rounded and it is used for crushing.

A lobster's skin is toughened by calcium salts, so it can be very hard and thick, giving good protection as well as acting as a skeleton for the animal. Like other crustaceans, a lobster has to shed its skin (molt) to grow, and even a large individual is in danger for a short time before the new skin hardens.

Lobsters chew their food well, using their pincers (if present), and the mouthparts around the mouth, to shred it. The food is then swallowed into the gizzard, which is a type of stomach with a tough lining where muscles help grind it more.

AN ARRAY OF SENSES
Lobsters have a pair of eyes, and two pairs of antennae. These are all prominent. Not quite so obvious are the thousands of tiny bristles over the body that work as sense organs. These detect chemicals and give a good sense of touch.

►The American spiny lobster takes part in spectacular mass migrations in the fall. Lobsters follow one behind the other in chains that may be up to 60 individuals long, keeping in touch with their antennae. As many as 100,000 may travel together, by both day and night, and they may cover 10mi in 24 hours.

▼*Jasus novaehollandiae* is a rock lobster from southern Australia. Like others of this group it has no pincers, but has a very spiny shell.

▶This crayfish, *Astacus pallipes*, hides under stones or in burrows in the riverbank during the day. At night it emerges and feeds on snails, worms and grubs.

▼▶The European spiny lobster (1) grows to 20in long. It is found in rocky crevices and stony places down to a depth of 230ft. *Scyllarides latus* (2) is a flattened lobster about 14in long with short legs. It lives on rocks, stones and sand. A European lobster, *Homarus gammarus* (3), in an aggressive pose. It lives among rocks and in crevices.

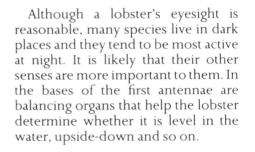

1

Although a lobster's eyesight is reasonable, many species live in dark places and they tend to be most active at night. It is likely that their other senses are more important to them. In the bases of the first antennae are balancing organs that help the lobster determine whether it is level in the water, upside-down and so on.

A STICKY BEGINNING
When lobsters mate, the male places sperm on the female's body near where her eggs will emerge – at the bases of the third legs. As the eggs are laid, they are fertilized. They then stick to the swimming legs on the female's abdomen, and stay there until they hatch. Each larva that emerges swims and feeds in the plankton and goes through many stages of development before it settles on the seabed to start its adult life.

DIVERSE HABITATS
Lobsters live offshore along most of the world's coasts, and some inhabit deep ocean waters down to 13,200ft.

There are also about 500 species found in fresh water, and these are known as crayfish. They are mostly around 4in long. Because they need calcium for their shells, they are most common in water with a high lime content. The European crayfish and the Red crayfish introduced to North America are typical, living concealed during the day and hunting at night. Sometimes they sit in burrows with just their antennae and claws protruding, waiting to grab prey.

In most respects, crayfish are very similar to sea lobsters, but they differ slightly in their breeding. They mate in the fall, and the female carries the eggs stuck under her tail through the winter. In late spring they hatch, not as larvae, but as tiny fully formed crayfish. It may be several years before they mature.

WANDERING MASSES
Spiny, or rock lobsters, live up to both of their names. They hide in dens between rocks, coming out to hunt. An individual may use several dens, hundreds of yards apart, that are within the area where it wanders as

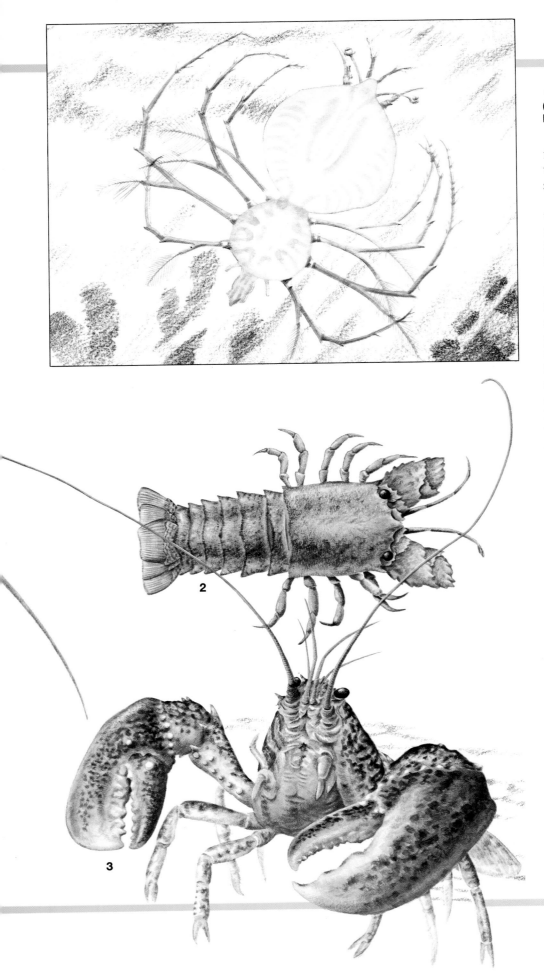

◄This delicate transparent floating larva (head pointing up) will turn into the spiny lobster shown opposite (1).

it hunts on the seabed. After a few weeks, the spiny lobster may move several miles to a new area.

Some spiny lobsters also migrate with the seasons. When the temperature drops in the fall, American spiny lobsters move south to a warmer area 30mi or more away.

COLOR CHANGE

Some species of lobster are naturally orange or red. These colors are often produced by pigments called carotenoids that are similar to those found in plants such as carrots. But many species of lobster, in life, are darker colors, such as the blue-black of the European lobster. Its color is due to the combination of a carotenoid pigment with a protein. When the lobster is cooked for eating, it turns red because the protein part of the color is broken down, leaving just the pure carotenoid showing.

LOBSTERS AS FOOD

People usually catch lobsters in traps, where they are drawn by a bait into a tunnel. This opens into a larger chamber from which they find it difficult to escape. The part of the lobster eaten is mainly the white meat of the large claw muscles and the other legs, and also the muscle of the abdomen.

The European common lobster and the American lobster are both caught in large numbers in cool waters. In warmer waters, many of the lobsters that are harvested commercially are spiny species. Freshwater crayfish are also good to eat, and are caught in several parts of the world. Scampi, which has become a popular seafood in recent years, is a kind of lobster. It is about 6in long, and it burrows in bottom mud. It is collected by dragging nets along the seabed (trawling).

HERMIT CRABS

As a girl peers into a rock pool, her shadow passes over the water. Nothing seems to be in the pool except a few lifeless shells. Then, when all is still, one of the shells scuttles away. Another moves, and, from its opening, some legs and antennae poke out. A hermit crab is living there. The girl moves. Quick as a flash, the crab pulls itself back in the shell and shuts the door.

Hermit crabs have an odd shape and odd habits, but nevertheless they are very successful. They can be seen on shores all over the world, and are found on the sea bottom. Some have even made a success of living most of the time on land. Within the same group of animals are the little porcelain crabs and the squat lobsters.

SECOND-HAND HOMES
The front part of a hermit crab has the same hard-shell cover, or carapace, found in other crabs and lobsters. This protects the head and trunk, and the legs and claws have a tough casing. The abdomen, though, is soft and unprotected. Hermit crabs, if they are to survive, must find a covering for the tail part of the body. They are adapted for a life inside the abandoned shells of shellfish such as winkles.

A hermit crab's abdomen is curled in such a way that it fits into a shell neatly. The legs on the abdomen are small, but one pair has hooks, so the crab can hold on to the shell without being dislodged. It can extend its legs from the shell to walk, carrying its home wherever it goes. If it is alarmed, it retreats far into the shell. Its pincers form a door for the shell, plugging the opening completely.

ALL CHANGE
Hermit crabs have to change shells as they grow. They are good at choosing one to fit, but in some places there is a shortage of shells and a crab may have to stay in a "house" that is small. Fights often occur between hermit crabs over the possession of a shell.

A hermit crab looking for a new shell will locate one by sight, then carefully investigate it. It takes hold of the shell with its walking legs and climbs on to it. If the shell feels right, the crab rotates it with its legs and explores it with its pincers. It pokes its claws into the shell to remove any sand or other debris. When the crab is satisfied, it climbs on the shell, and swiftly transfers its abdomen from the old to the new shell.

Not all hermit crabs live in the shells of sea snails. Some, including deep-sea species that can live as much as 16,500ft beneath the surface, live in tusk shells. Others live in coral, or holes in wood or stone.

HERMIT CRABS
Infraorder Anomura (*several hundred species*)

Habitat: sea bottom; some on land.

Diet: meat-eating scavengers, or filter feeders; some plant-eaters.

Breeding: sexes separate; females carry fertilized eggs; larval stages in plankton.

Distribution: worldwide.

Size: carapace (head-thorax shell) up to 8in long; longer overall, but abdomen often twisted.

Color: very varied.

Species mentioned in text:
Broad-clawed porcelain crab (*Porcellana platycheles*)
Coconut crab (*Birgus latro*)
Common hermit crab (*Pagurus bernhardus*)
Mole crab (e.g., *Emerita talpoida*)
Squat lobster (e.g., *Galathea strigosa*)

◄This hermit crab is house-hunting; it has grown too big for its shell and is testing another to see if it is the correct size to fit.

LIVING IN HARMONY

Various kinds of hermit crab live in association with completely different animals. The species *Pagurus prideauxi*, for example, forms a partnership with a sea anemone, *Adamsia carcinopados*. The anemone grows to completely cover the small shell inhabited by the young crab. As the crab grows, the horny base of the anemone grows too, forming a "shell" for the crab which gives all-around protection. The crab benefits from the protection of the anemone's stinging tentacles. The anemone gets food particles as the crab tears up meat to eat.

Another association is often seen between the Common hermit crab and the Parasitic anemone. Again the anemone gives protection and gets

▼In the water off the Cape coast of South Africa a hermit crab is camouflaged by its sponge covering.

►Large specimens of the Common hermit crab of European coasts often find a home in the shell of a whelk.

food scraps in return. It is not a parasite, in spite of its name. The hermit crab favors old whelk shells, and so does the anemone. There can be several anemones on one shell. Although this arrangement can benefit both partners, the crab can live without the anemone and vice versa. There may be a third partner in the association, a ragworm, *Nereis fucata*, which lives in the whelk shell alongside the hermit crab.

Hermit crabs may also live with sponges. The orange sponge *Suberites domuncula* often settles on whelk shells that contain hermit crabs. The sponge may dissolve these shells away, but its large rounded mass provides the crabs with a home instead.

FEEDING HABITS
Hermit crabs often catch small prey such as small fish. They also scavenge for dead animals and plants. However, many kinds feed for much of the time on food particles within deposits of sand or mud. They scoop the sand up, usually with their smaller pincers, and then sort and sift it using their mouthparts. They swallow any edible morsels. This kind of feeding can sustain hermit crabs for long periods even in the depths of the sea.

LAND HERMITS
In the tropics, some hermit crabs have become largely land-living, ranging inland from the upper shore. They may use as homes the shells of land snails. All species must return to the water for breeding, as their larvae are the typical crab planktonic type.

Perhaps the most remarkable of the land hermits is the Coconut crab. Young adults make their homes in empty snail shells, but they gradually outgrow those that are available. They

◄This hermit crab has made its home in an old whelk shell with several individuals of the "parasitic" anemone *Calliactis parasitica* growing on it.

may then carry on their backs half of a coconut shell for protection. Eventually, not even these shells are large enough for such big crabs; they grow to 6in across. Each crab then relies on its claws and tough skin for protection. It holds its abdomen tucked under the body.

NUT-CRACKER
A fully grown Coconut crab can put its legs around the trunk of a palm tree. It climbs well and, using its strong pincers, can pull off coconuts. It hammers and cracks open the shell then eats the flesh. It feeds on other fruits too, and on dead animals.

The Coconut crab lives in burrows that it digs out under tree roots and lines with fibers from coconuts. Its gills are reduced, but it has a chamber lined with a network of blood vessels that works as a lung.

MIXED RELATIONS
Squat lobsters look, as their name suggests, like short round lobsters with tails flexed underneath the body. In fact, they are more closely related to hermit crabs than to true lobsters. Porcelain crabs look at first glance like true crabs, but they have long antennae. In all species of hermit crab, squat lobster and porcelain crab the fifth pair of walking legs are very small.

Squat lobsters sift sand and mud for food. Some are found close to shore, but there are over 100 species that live in deep waters, some going down to 13,000ft. Inshore forms often hide in crevices in rocks and among stones. Some are brightly colored.

Most porcelain crabs are small. The Broad-clawed porcelain crab lives among the seaweeds and rocks near the low-water mark along European coasts. It is only ½in long.

The mole crabs are another group of small hermit crab relatives. They grow to about 2in long. They are filter feeders that burrow into sand by flexing their abdomens.

CRABS

The tropical beach seems deserted as two picnickers arrive on the sand. But once they are still, crabs emerge from hundreds of holes dotted across the beach. They go about their business, gathering small balls of wet sand, or waving their claws at one another. Then, as one of the picnickers moves, all the crabs dive underground.

The familiar beach crabs, along with spider crabs, are classed as true crabs. Typically, they are meat-eaters, either as predators or as scavengers, and they spend most of their time walking on the sea bottom. (For other types of crabs see pages 50-53, 58-59.)

All the true crabs have a small symmetrical abdomen, which is held folded under the body out of sight. The antennae are usually short. The shell, called the carapace, covers the combined head and thorax regions (the cephalothorax), extends sideways, and the walking legs are under it. The first pair of walking legs have grasping claws, and in some species these "pincers" are huge. The other four pairs of legs are used for walking rather than grasping food.

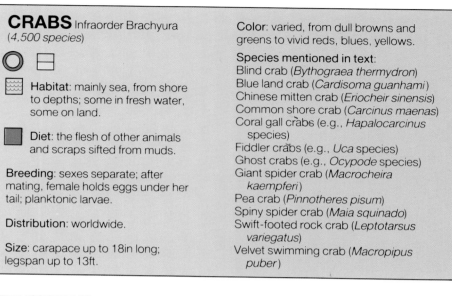

CRABS Infraorder Brachyura
(4,500 species)

Habitat: mainly sea, from shore to depths; some in fresh water, some on land.

Diet: the flesh of other animals and scraps sifted from muds.

Breeding: sexes separate; after mating, female holds eggs under her tail; planktonic larvae.

Distribution: worldwide.

Size: carapace up to 18in long; legspan up to 13ft.

Color: varied, from dull browns and greens to vivid reds, blues, yellows.

Species mentioned in text:
Blind crab (*Bythograea thermydron*)
Blue land crab (*Cardisoma guanhami*)
Chinese mitten crab (*Eriocheir sinensis*)
Common shore crab (*Carcinus maenas*)
Coral gall crabs (e.g., *Hapalocarcinus* species)
Fiddler crabs (e.g., *Uca* species)
Ghost crabs (e.g., *Ocypode* species)
Giant spider crab (*Macrocheira kaempferi*)
Pea crab (*Pinnotheres pisum*)
Spiny spider crab (*Maia squinado*)
Swift-footed rock crab (*Leptotarsus variegatus*)
Velvet swimming crab (*Macropipus puber*)

SIDE-STEPPING

With their walking legs positioned beneath their bodies, crabs can balance well. Many of them are able to move fast over the seabed or beach. Species such as ghost crabs can run so fast that most predators find them difficult to catch. But nearly all crabs move sideways. This way they can bend and stretch each leg quickly without tripping over the others.

Some crabs have become specialist swimmers, with the last pair of legs modified into flattened paddles. One such species that may be encountered on European shores is the Velvet swimming crab. The joints of its legs are blue, and its back legs are flattened and hairy. This crab is small – the carapace grows to only about 3in in length – but it is short-tempered and is liable to nip hard if disturbed.

SEA- AND RIVER-DWELLERS

Many crabs live on the sea bottom around coasts. But relatively few crabs live in the real sea depths, perhaps because of a shortage of food there. One unusual deep-sea species is the Blind crab. This is a predator in areas surrounding hot vents – undersea "volcanoes" – which give out thick sulfurous material 1½mi below the sea surface. Here the temperature may be 62°F rather than the usual deep-sea chill of only 37 or 39°F.

In the tropics, several crab species live in only fresh water. In Europe, the Common shore crab lives in estuaries as well as the sea. Another crab that may be found in European rivers is the Chinese mitten crab. This grows to about 2in long, and gets its name from its furry pincers. It is an Asian species, but early this century some

◀A Swift-footed rock crab of Australia feeds at night at low tide.

◄A ghost crab seeks refuge from enemies by burrowing in the sand. Only its large eyes protrude to keep watch.

▲Fiddler crabs use their large nippers in ritual combat. Here two males of the genus *Uca* test their strength.

individuals got carried on cargo ships to several European rivers. It can make itself a nuisance by burrowing in banks, which then collapse. It lives in fresh water, but goes down to the sea to breed.

LANDLUBBERS

Also in the tropics, some species are adapted to life on land. These land crabs may live 1mi or more from the sea, spending the day hiding under stones and emerging when the Sun

goes down. At breeding time, they make mass migrations to the sea. These species, and some of the ghost crabs, may actually drown if forced to remain underwater for too long.

Fiddler crabs live at the top of muddy or sandy tropical shores. Each crab has its own burrow, which it defends against others of its kind. The male has one of its claws enormously developed, and constantly waves it with a beckoning gesture. It serves to both intimidate rivals and attract females. Sometimes whole beaches are covered with the burrows of thousands of these crabs. They pick up pellets of sand or mud, and scrape off tiny food organisms with special hairs on their mouthparts.

LITTLE AND LARGE

Among the smaller crabs is the aptly named Pea crab. Its body is spherical and ⅔in across. Females are larger than males. These crabs live inside mussels and oysters, stealing food filtered from the water by the mollusc.

Female coral gall crabs become prisoners in their own homes. Their shells become surrounded by growing coral, so that they are left with a hole just large enough for plankton food to enter and for the tiny male to get in for mating.

Spider crabs are long-legged, but they are generally slow-moving. They are often encrusted with seaweeds,

▼As it shows off the large colored claw that it uses for displays, this fiddler crab is "blinking" with one eye.

▶The Blue land crab *Cardisoma guanhami* climbs trees in search of prey. One pincer is larger than the other.

sponges and other organisms that together help the crabs' camouflage. Some spider crabs are tiny, with a carapace only ⅔in long, but the Spiny spider crab of Europe may span 7in long. However, this is dwarfed by the Giant spider crab, which has a carapace 18in long and 12in across, and extremely wide-spreading legs. The furthest distance between the tips of the legs may be 13ft. The crab can inflict a nasty wound on a person. This giant is known only from a small area off the coast of Japan. The few individuals that are caught by fishing boats are used for food.

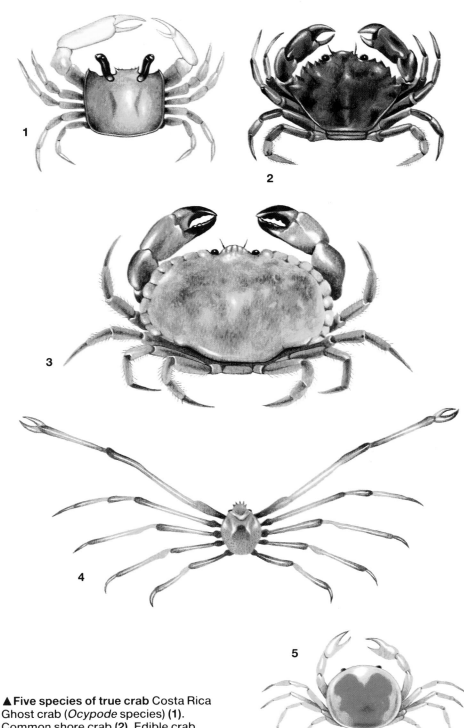

▲Five species of true crab Costa Rica Ghost crab (*Ocypode* species) (1). Common shore crab (2). Edible crab (*Cancer pagurus*) (3). Giant spider crab (4), with legs outstretched. Its pincers may be held 10ft apart. Pea crab (*Pinnotheres* species) (5). (Not to scale.)

HORSESHOE CRABS

It is springtime. Tonight, on the Atlantic coast of North America, there is a full Moon and high tides. As the tide comes high up the little beach, the moonlight glints on the backs of rounded shapes at the water's edge. The shapes are moving, a seething mass of horseshoe crabs. They are taking part in a mating ritual that has happened here every spring for millions of years.

Horseshoe crabs, also known as king crabs, are not crabs at all. They are not even crustaceans, being more closely related to spiders and scorpions.

HINGED SHELL

Horseshoe crabs have a shell that completely covers their backs for protection. It is hinged so that the rear part moves independently. A long tail spine sticks out behind the shell. The front part of the shell has an outline like a horseshoe, giving these animals their name. From above, few features can be seen, but there is a pair of bean-shaped compound eyes on each side of the highest point of the shell.

Viewed from below, the five pairs of walking legs can be seen, each with small pincers on the end. In front of these are a small pair of mouthparts with pincers which the animal uses to grab food. Under the rear of the body are limbs that have become modified into "gill books." Each of these has 200 little leaflets, through which oxygen is extracted from the water. Muscles can flap these gill books to help with breathing. Sometimes the gill books are used as paddles for swimming.

DIGGING IN THE SAND

Horseshoe crabs spend most of their time burrowing in the surface of sand or mud, feeding on prey such as worms and shellfish. The last (fifth) pair of walking legs are specially adapted as shovels. There are spiny extensions on the body end of the walking legs that stick into the mouth and act as jaws. The long tail spine seems to have little function, but the crab uses it to right itself if it gets turned over accidentally.

EGG-LAYING

During the breeding season, egg-laying takes place when there is a very high tide at night. Thousands, perhaps millions, of horseshoe crabs emerge at the edge of the sea. The females, which are the larger sex, are followed, or clung to, by the males. At the very top of the tide the females stop, dig a hole and lay their eggs. The males fertilize the eggs immediately. The action of the waves buries many of the eggs in the sand, where they stand the best chance of surviving.

After several months, when another high tide covers them, the 1in-long larvae emerge and swim away. They resemble the trilobites that swam in the sea millions of years ago. They take 3 years to reach adulthood.

▲ An upside-down horseshoe crab displays its walking legs and the hind limbs with their gill books, which extract oxygen from the water.

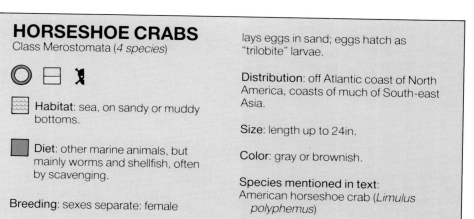

HORSESHOE CRABS
Class Merostomata (*4 species*)

Habitat: sea, on sandy or muddy bottoms.

Diet: other marine animals, but mainly worms and shellfish, often by scavenging.

Breeding: sexes separate: female lays eggs in sand; eggs hatch as "trilobite" larvae.

Distribution: off Atlantic coast of North America, coasts of much of South-east Asia.

Size: length up to 24in.

Color: gray or brownish.

Species mentioned in text: American horseshoe crab (*Limulus polyphemus*)

▲American horseshoe crabs gather at high tide for mating. Apart from these gatherings, horseshoe crabs are rarely seen as they burrow in the mud in deep water off the coast.

►Animals almost identical to the present-day horseshoe crabs were living 180 million years ago. In past ages there were many kinds of horseshoe crab. Now only four species survive.

SLUGS, SNAILS

The tide is in. A Dog whelk glides slowly along looking for prey. It tastes the water to home in on food. On these rocks there is rarely far to travel for a meal. It comes up against a barnacle. The barnacle closes its shell for protection. But the Dog whelk simply bores a hole in the barnacle shell to get at its edible insides.

The whelks, slugs, snails and their relations are the most numerous of all groups of molluscs. The molluscs are one of the most successful groups of invertebrates, with about 100,000 species altogether. Nearly two-thirds are snail-like.

SOFT BODY, HARD SHELL

A mollusc's body is soft, and usually divided into a head, a muscular foot, and a visceral hump with a mantle on top. Sense organs and nerves are concentrated in the head, and the hump contains the other main body organs. There are no paired legs. Although the body is soft, most molluscs are well protected by a hard chalky shell.

The group of molluscs that includes the slugs and snails is called Gastropoda. The name means belly-feet, and describes the position of the broad muscular foot beneath the body. The animals creep on this, secreting a carpet of slime on which to move. As well as being numerous, gastropods are widespread. They are found in all kinds of climates, and not only in the sea and in fresh water, but on land, too, where they are the only molluscs. But their skins are thin and moist, and they prefer damp places.

▼These tropical slugs of the genus *Trichotoxon* may go through a courtship ritual several hours long before mating.

SLUGS, SNAILS
Class Gastropoda (*60,000 species*)

○ ⊟ ✗

◨ Habitat: seas, fresh water and on land.

◪ Diet: very varied; includes plant-eaters and meat-eaters, also filter-feeders and parasites.

Breeding: sexes separate in some, but others have both sexes in one animal; planktonic larvae in aquatic forms.

Distribution: worldwide.

Size: length 1/25 to 30in.

Color: species occur in almost every imaginable color.

Species mentioned in text:
Abalone (*Haliotis* species)
African land snail (*Achatina* species)
Banana slug (*Ariolimax californicus*)
Common limpet (*Patella vulgata*)
Cone shell (*Conus* species)
Cowrie (*Cypraea* species)
Dog whelk (*Nucella lapillus*)
European whelk (*Buccinum undatum*)
Garden snail (*Helix aspersa*)
Helmet shell (*Phalium labiatum*)
Murex snail (*Murex brandaris*)
Necklace shell (*Natica alderi*)
Pink conch (*Strombus gigas*)
Roman snail (*Helix pomatia*)
Sea lemon (e.g., *Archidoris pseudoargus*)
Sea slug (e.g., *Dendronotus* species)
Shelled slug (*Testacella* species)
Slug (e.g., *Limax* species)
Top shell (e.g., *Gibbula* species)

In the gastropod group are the land snails and slugs, freshwater snails, sea slugs, limpets, and a host of sea snails, including whelks, periwinkles, cone shells, conches, and cowries.

MANTLE OF SUCCESS

The mantle consists of a fold of skin. It covers and protects the digestive, blood circulatory, reproductive and excretory systems and such structures as the gills and some mucus secreting glands. In some gastropods, such as the Garden snail and many other land and freshwater snails, there are no gills. Instead the pocket formed between mantle and body functions as a lung. The skin of the mantle can secrete a variety of substances. Its thickened edge has many gland cells, and these secrete the shell.

A gastropod adds to its shell as its body grows. New growth occurs at the shell lip, and only limited repairs can be made to the shell should it become damaged elsewhere. Sometimes lines can be seen on a shell where growth has been interrupted

▶ Although each is both male and female, these Roman snails mate in pairs, so fertilizing one another.

▼ In front of this Helmet shell are two tentacles with eyes at the base. The breathing siphon that takes in sea water rises up behind them.

by cold or drought. The shell is mostly made of calcium carbonate, the main part of chalk rock. This chemical is laid down in layers that slant at different angles, giving extra strength.

THE RIGHT WAY TO COIL

Gastropod shells come in a great variety of shapes and thicknesses. Sea snails often have thick and heavy shells. Their land relatives, with no water to support their weight, tend to have thinner shells. The shell surface may be textured or sculptured in many different ways.

In most gastropods the shell is spirally coiled. Shells range from tall, narrow and pointed to flat and disc-like. In nearly all species the shell coils in the same direction – counter-clock-wise from above. A few individuals may be found with their shell coiling the opposite way. A very small number of species show the "wrong" sort of coiling, and a tiny number have shells that may be coiled in either direction.

DOORS AND PLUGS

Many of the sea snails have a horny lid for their shells. A flat round plate, the operculum, is secreted by the rear of the foot. When the animal retreats into its shell it is the last part pulled in, and it blocks the entrance like a trapdoor. It keeps out predators, and in shore species it also prevents water loss. Land snails such as the Garden snail do not have a horny lid, but if they retreat into their shells to shelter from bad weather, they often seal themselves in with a waterproof plug of hardened mucus.

Lids are different shapes to fit the different shell entrances. In several species, such as the Pink conch shell, there are "teeth" on the operculum to deter predators.

FEEDING TACTICS

Snails and their relatives all use for feeding an organ called a radula. This is a type of tongue covered in rows of little teeth. It works similar to a file, to rasp off pieces of food that are then swallowed. The radula is surrounded by muscles that can move it back and forth and from side to side. It grows continuously at the base with new rows of teeth. Old teeth wear and fall off from the front.

The radula has a different pattern in different types of gastropod. Plant-eaters, such as land snails and slugs,

▲ Hundreds of little teeth cover the radula of a top shell, and rasp the plants that the animal eats. Gastropods that eat meat have fewer, but larger, teeth. All snails and their relatives have a file-like radula in their mouths to help them eat.

▼ A Banana slug grips a twig with its slimy body as it climbs. Slugs are snails with small shells or none at all.

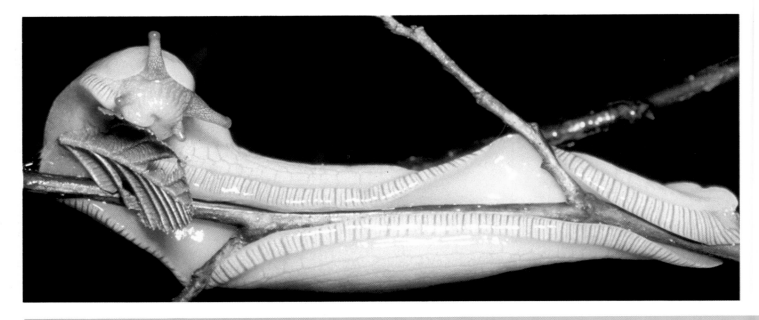

have a broad radula with many small teeth. When the animals are feeding, you can hear them rasping away at plants. Limpets browse small plants from the rocks on the seashore, and they have a hard rasping radula with a few strong teeth in each row. They leave scratch marks on rock surfaces.

Some minute sea slugs have a very small radula with teeth that pierce individual cells of tiny, thread-like plants to get at their contents.

POISONS AND ACIDS

Meat-eating gastropods, for example whelks, often have a narrow radula with a few teeth, but each tooth has long pointed cusps. The cone shells of warm seas, which are fierce predators, have large teeth developed as a kind of harpoon. They jab into prey, such as fish and worms, and inject a deadly paralyzing poison, before swallowing them whole. Cone shells can give a painful jab to humans, and some of the tropical species can kill a person.

Less deadly, but more sneaky, are the habits of such sea snails as dog whelks and necklace shells. These attack static prey that includes barnacles and clams. They bore holes through the shells with their radula to extract the body contents. Necklace shells also secrete an acid that softens the shell under attack.

Many of the meat-eaters have a shell with a groove that opens at the front for the siphon. The siphon is a tube formed from part of the mantle edge. It carries water to the gills in the mantle cavity, and also contains a chemical sense organ. The gastropod can use its siphon as a sort of nose to follow the scent of prey or carrion.

LIFE WITHOUT A SHELL

Slugs are just snails without a shell, although many in fact do have small remnant shells. There are two main groups of slug-type gastropods, one on the land and one in the sea. They are not closely related.

▲ Triton shells are among the largest of all snails. They are fierce predators found in the sea. This one, *Charonia nodifera*, is beginning to eat a starfish.

▼ Most sea slugs are meat-eaters that "graze" on animals that cannot escape. Here some *Polycera quadrilineata* work their way across a sea mat colony.

▲Molluscs of mainly North European coasts The sea hare, *Aplysia* species **(1)**, lives among weed in shallow waters. If disturbed it ejects purple dye. The Dog whelk **(2)** lives on the middle shore, feeding on barnacles. The European whelk **(3)** lives down to depths of 330ft in the sea on sand and mud. *Neopilina* **(4)** is a limpet-like mollusc found in the ocean depths. The Common limpet **(5)** lives on rocks. When the tide is in it moves around to feed. The Flat periwinkle (*Littorina littoralis*) **(6)** lives on seaweeds, well disguised from predators by its color and shape.

▶In cowries, such as this Australian species, the soft tissues of its insides (the mantle) grow over and wrap round the shell. The animals hunt at night along the coral reef.

Land slugs are mainly plant-eaters. Like many snails, they tend to feed on dying or rotting vegetation rather than healthy plants, but some kinds can be pests in gardens or fields if their numbers build up. The shelled slugs, which carry a tiny shell on their tails, are land species with a different diet. They eat earthworms and pursue them underground.

Most of the sea slugs eat small marine animals, particularly kinds that encrust rocks and reefs. They mostly move by crawling on the foot. Some sea slugs, though, are active swimmers, and catch food in the plankton. Some feed on jellyfish, swallowing the jellyfish's stinging cells whole and transferring them to their own skins. There they give the slug protection just as they did the original owner.

BEAUTIFUL BODIES

Unlike land slugs, which win no beauty prizes, the sea slugs include

▼ One of the sea lemon family of sea slugs. Some of this family can defend themselves by squirting acid.

some of the most beautiful marine animals. They come in a huge variety of colors. Some are camouflaged, but others are dazzling reds, yellow and other brilliant colors and patterns. Several of these colors may each warn possible attackers that the slug tastes nasty, but in many species the reason for the colors is not understood. A number of the brightest species live deep in the sea where it is too dark to see them anyway.

Many kinds of sea slug have extra adornments in the feathery gills covering their backs. The true gills are absent, but these frilly outgrowths help the animals gather oxygen.

LOVE DARTS

The sea snails and limpets have separate sexes, but the sea slugs and the land snails and slugs have both sexes in the same animal. Even so, each seeks out another individual to mate with. In some slugs and snails courtship is elaborate. For example, several species of slug mate dangling from plants on a rope of slime they have made themselves. In snails such as the

Garden snail, the pair "shoot" each other with a hard dart of lime to trigger exchange of sperms.

After mating, winkles and freshwater snails lay large clutches of small eggs in a mass of jelly attached to plants. Sea slugs lay a ribbon of eggs, and whelks leave their eggs in leathery capsules attached to rocks. Land snails often bury their eggs in the soil.

Some gastropod eggs are transparent. Others have a limy shell. The eggs of the large African snail *Archachatina marginata* look like small bird's eggs. Land and freshwater snails' eggs hatch as little snails, but in sea gastropods there is a planktonic larval stage before the animal settles down.

SNAILS AND MAN

Many kinds of sea snail are used by people as food, from periwinkles to abalones. Some land snails, too, are good to eat. The Roman snail is a European species much favored, but now scarce in some of its former haunts. Some slugs are pests, as are giant African land snails which people have spread to Asia and the Pacific.

CLAMS, MUSSELS

A group of scallops is resting on the sea floor. An enemy, a starfish, moves stealthily towards one. Just before it touches its quarry, the scallop shoots up into the water and swims off, clapping its shells together and making jets of water that push it out of trouble. Once out of range, it settles on the seabed, but keeps its senses alert.

Fast active movement is not typical of the majority of clams and mussels. Many spend much of their adult life immobile, or they move only slowly. Most live in the sea, but there are many freshwater species, too. They belong to the group known as bivalves, meaning two-shells. All have a double shell, secreted by a two-lobed body hump. The two shells fit together tightly, and the animal can retreat inside this covering to protect itself from its enemies.

SPRINGY HINGE

A bivalve's two shells are joined at a hinge point. Often, hinge "teeth" in one shell fit into corresponding sockets in the other. A horny ligament also connects the shells, and this pulls on the hinge. The shells are pulled together, when necessary, by blocks of muscles running between them.

In an empty shell you can often see the scars where the muscle blocks were attached. Because muscles keep the shells closed, when the animal dies the shells open up. Soon the horny hinge rots. This is why empty shells on the shore are usually found singly and not hinged in pairs.

PEARLY SECRETIONS

Each shell is composed of several layers. The innermost one is often shiny with a colored sheen. This is called mother-of-pearl, and this part of the shell is sometimes used by people for decorative purposes. At one time there was a large industry

CLAMS, MUSSELS
Class Bivalvia (*15,000 species*)

Habitat: mainly seas; also brackish and fresh water.

Diet: small food items strained from water or sifted from mud.

Breeding: shed eggs and sperm into water; larvae in plankton before settling down.

Distribution: worldwide.

Size: shell length ⅕in to 60in.

Color: shell often dull, but colored or patterned in some; soft parts may be brightly colored.

Species mentioned in text:
Blunt tellin (*Tellina crassa*)
Common or Edible mussel (*Mytilus edulis*)
Common piddock (*Pholas dactylus*)
Freshwater mussel (e.g., *Unio pictorum*)
Giant clam (*Tridacna gigas*)
Great scallop (*Pecten maximus*)
Oyster (e.g., *Ostrea edulis*)
Pearl mussel (*Margaritifera margaritifera*)
Razor shell (e.g., *Ensis siliqua*)
Sand gaper (*Mya arenaria*)
Shipworm (*Teredo navalis*)
Zebra mussel (*Dreissena polymorpha*)

◄ In bivalves such as mussels, water enters one siphon (frilled, below) and leaves by another (above). On the way, food and oxygen are taken from it.

▼ Tentacles sensitive to touch fringe the mantle at the edge of a scallop's shell.

making mother-of-pearl buttons from freshwater mussels.

The familiar spherical pearls are made of the same substance as the inner part of a bivalve's shell. They are made around any small object which has entered the animal. Often this is a small parasite. The flesh of the bivalve's mantle reacts to the foreign tissue by secreting pearl substance in order to seal off the parasite from its body. A string of pearls on someone's neck is simply a collection of secretions around dead parasites.

HELPING NATURE ALONG
Pearls may form in many sorts of bivalve. They are common in freshwater mussels, but in these species they are usually tiny and may be oddly shaped. The Pearl mussel is a large freshwater species up to 6in long. It lives, and is fished for, in fast-flowing rivers in the Northern Hemisphere. It produces large, good-quality pearls.

Marine oysters are also a recognized source of pearls, and some people dive after them for a living. Oyster pearls can be cultured (encouraged to form) by introducing a tiny pearl as a "seed" into the animals, which may then deposit more pearl layers. By the time the oysters are harvested, the pearls are commercially useful.

A SNAIL-LIKE BODY PLAN
Although rather different from snails in appearance, clams and other bivalves show some similarities (see pages 60-61). They have a large fleshy mantle covering the body, and this secretes the shells. They have a muscular foot. This is tiny in some species, but large and important in others, although it is never used for creeping on like a snail.

There is very little in a bivalve, though, that could be called a head. A mouth, surrounded by a pair of fleshy lobes, leads into the digestive system,

▲ The Giant clam houses tiny plants in the edge of its mantle. These make food that is used by the clam, which provides shelter for these small partners.

but there are no tentacles or eyes on the head. When they are present, they are located on the mantle. A bivalve has no radula (rasping tongue) either, and this gives a clue to its eating habits.

FEEDING BY FILTER
Most bivalves have enormous gills, and these serve two purposes: to get oxygen into the body, and to trap tiny food items in the water.

In feeding, the gills act as both a net and separator. Large particles, such as lumps of sand, are separated out and allowed to drop away. Microscopic plants in the water are trapped by cilia (tiny hairs), wrapped in mucus, then passed down special grooved pathways with beating cilia to the mouth, where this food is swallowed.

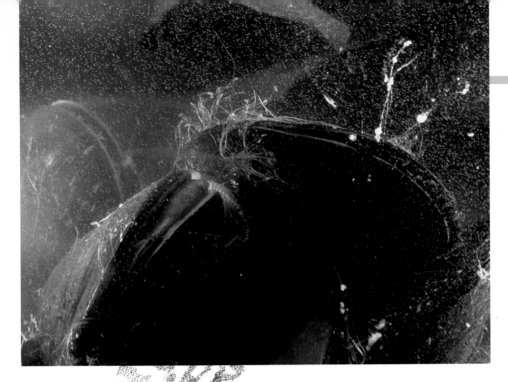

Many bivalves have part of the mantle elongated into a siphon or tube to act as a water channel. Most have an inlet and an outlet siphon. The inlet siphon often bears tentacles and sense cells to monitor the incoming water. In several species these siphons are short, but in burrowing forms, such as the Blunt tellin, they can be extended to several times the length of the shell. The inlet siphon is used to grope about on the sand surface, sucking in possible food.

BORERS AND BURROWERS

Several kinds of bivalve are able to bore into rock. The Common piddock pushes out its round foot to grip the rock ahead of it, then rotates its shell back and forth. The shell has sharp spiny ridges that act as files to wear away the rock. The piddock lives in the cavity it makes in the rock, but filters the surrounding water for food.

▲ Clouds of eggs and sperm are released by Edible mussels at breeding time. Fertilization takes place in the water. Out of thousands of offspring produced, only a few survive their larval stages. They swim in the plankton until ready to settle, then never travel again.

◀▲ Some species of bivalve The Common mussel (1) is up to 4in long. It lives attached by strong threads to rocks on the lower shore. Huge numbers are eaten by predators, including humans and birds such as oystercatchers. The Sand gaper (2) grows to 6in long. It burrows in mud and sand. The Giant clam (3) is a tropical species that grows up to 5ft in length.

The shipworm is a bivalve that bores into wood. Its body is long and thin (hence the name worm), with the shell reduced to function just as a boring tool. Shipworms live in floating timber, wooden piers, and in the timbers of wooden boats. Not only is the wood a place to live, it also provides some food, as shipworms can digest timber.

Among the many bivalves that live buried in sand or mud are the gapers, or soft-shell clams. These live 12in or more below the surface, putting up their siphons to collect food. They do not move around much. Other species are active burrowers. Razor shells, with their long tubular shells, have a very powerful foot and can move rapidly through the sand. When bivalves burrow, they push out the foot, then pump it up with blood so it provides a firm footing to pull along the rest of the body.

STAYING STILL

For many bivalves it is not necessary to move at all, and they may be fixed to one spot. The Common mussel is attached to rocks on the shore by strong threads of a silk-like substance that grow from near its hinge. The freshwater Zebra mussel, which lives mainly in Asia, also anchors itself with threads. But these animals still can, at times, detach themselves and move slowly using the foot.

Some oysters are more firmly glued to the ground beneath. Giant clams are also stationary. During their long lives, as they grow so too may the coral on the reef around them. Eventually they become firmly fixed in a pocket of reef.

A FISH TO HANG ON TO

Seawater bivalves release their sperm and eggs into the water. The resulting larvae live in the plankton before settling down. In freshwater cockles and pea mussels there is a relatively small number of larvae, and these are brooded inside the mother, to be released as tiny adults.

Freshwater mussels have an odd life history in which the larvae are brooded over the winter by the mother, then released in spring. The larvae float away, each with a sticky thread attached to it. They cannot swim, but should any of them come in contact with a fish, such as a stickleback, the thread catches on to it. The larva attaches itself to the fish's skin, and stays embedded there for several weeks, feeding on blood and mucus. As a small mussel, it drops to the bottom of the pond or stream, where it spends the rest of its life.

▼Tiny black eyes sit along the mantle fringe of the Great scallop. It detects predators by sight and smell.

OCTOPUS, SQUID, CUTTLEFISH

A shape emerges from a crevice between two rocks. It flows across the seabed, changing the whole time, with sometimes a suckered arm reaching out in front. It is an octopus hunting. It has seen a crab. It moves stealthily towards it. As the octopus approaches its meal, it suddenly changes color from a drab greenish-brown to dark red. It gathers itself in. Then the crab moves, and it pounces. It folds the crab in its arms and bites it with its beak.

Octopuses, together with cuttlefish, squids and their relations make up the group of animals called cephalopods ("head-feet"). They are molluscs (see pages 60-61), but look very different from the static clams or slow-moving snails. Cephalopods are active hunters. Some are among the fastest of all creatures in the sea over short distances. They also include the biggest of the invertebrates, and those with probably the most efficient sense organs and brains.

ARM AND SHELL VARIATIONS

The great majority of cephalopods are squids of various kinds. Most are highly active, torpedo-shaped and built for fast swimming. Many travel in shoals, and they move too quickly to be easily caught in nets. They have ten long arms.

Cuttlefish also have ten arms, but these are usually rather small and flattened. They often live close to, or buried in, the sea floor. They have an internal shell, the cuttlebone, which when they die washes up on to beaches and is used by bird-keepers to provide calcium for their pets. Many squids have an internal shell too, but it is often just a small horny stiffening bar.

Octopuses, as the name (derived from Greek) indicates, have eight legs. They usually stay near the seabed, and are the least active of cephalopods, hiding in the rocks and catching slow-moving prey. They have no shell.

The pearly nautiluses are the only living cephalopods with a hard outer shell. They are the most ancient of cephalopods, and have existed for hundreds of millions of years.

ARMS ON ITS FOOT

In cephalopods, the muscular foot of other molluscs such as the snails has become a ring of tentacles, the arms, around the mouth. The arms have

▶ A prey's eye view of a Pacific octopus (*Octopus dofleini*) off the coast of Oregon. This animal is usually mottled brown or grayish-yellow, but when it is excited it flushes red.

OCTOPUS, SQUID, CUTTLEFISH Class
Cephalopoda (*650 species*)

○ □

Habitat: sea, often near surface.

Diet: fish, shellfish.

Breeding: internal fertilization; lay eggs; emerging young resemble parents.

Distribution: worldwide.

Size: length from about 2in to 65ft.

Color: very varied; browns, reds, white. Some capable of much color change.

Species mentioned in text:
Blue-ringed octopus (*Hapalochlaena maculosa*)
Common cuttlefish (*Sepia officinalis*)
Common octopus (*Octopus vulgaris*)
Common pearly nautilus (*Nautilus pompilius*)
Giant squid (*Architeuthis harveyi*)
Lesser octopus (*Eledone cirrhosa*)
Little cuttlefish (*Sepiola atlantica*)

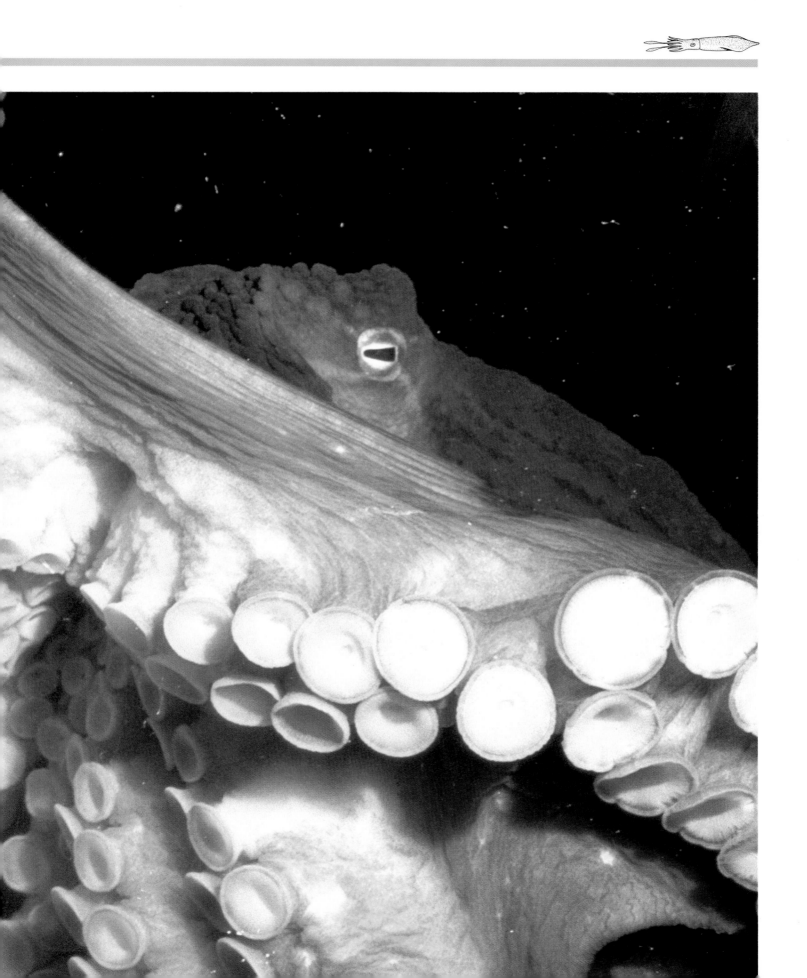

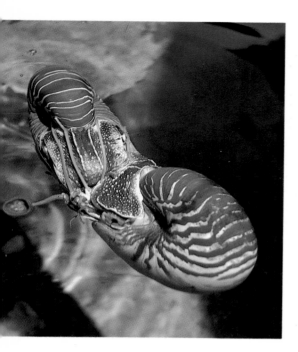

▲The pearly nautiluses live in the tropical waters of the Indian and Pacific oceans. Here a pair are mating.

▼The Little cuttle grows to only 2in long. It swims using a bird-like flapping of its short, wide, side fins. Sometimes it burrows in the sand.

suckers on them that can grasp prey. In some species of squid the suckers have sharp claws to help in the task. At the entrance to the mouth is a hard horny beak. This can bite into hard prey, for example crabs. Many cephalopods can inject poison as they bite, and kill prey such as crustaceans even quicker. The Blue-ringed octopus, a small tropical species, has a bite that can kill a person.

As well as the mouth, the head bears two large eyes. Like humans, cephalopods seem to be creatures that rely mainly on eyesight. They also have a very large (for an invertebrate) brain, which may have protecting gristle around it.

Behind the head is the body region, which contains the digestive system and reproductive organs. As in other molluscs, it is covered by a mantle. In the mantle cavity are large gills. The lower edge of the mantle cavity is drawn out into a funnel. This plays an important part in cephalopod life. When the mantle cavity walls relax, water is drawn in. When the walls contract, water can be ejected quickly through the funnel. This gives the useful option of jet propulsion when the animal needs to travel fast.

CATCHING A MEAL

Squid often rely on their speed to catch food, and can take fast-moving fish like mackerel. Two of the ten arms are specially developed for prey capture. They can be folded back to the head, then suddenly shot out to grasp food and bring it to the mouth.

Cuttlefish search for prey such as shrimps on the seabed, blowing water out of their funnels to uncover buried individuals. A cuttlefish may have to back off to get its prey-catching arms to the right distance to be shot out.

Octopuses have no special arms for capturing animals, and they "jump" on to their victims. The Common octopus can be a greedy feeder. In captivity it may eat 20 to 30 crabs a day.

AN ARRAY OF SENSES

The eyes of the primitive nautiluses are little more than poor pin-hole cameras, but an octopus's eyes are strikingly like ours in their build. Each has a lens and very sensitive retina. Tests show that an octopus is capable of seeing extremely well and can detect some types of light, such as polarized light, that we cannot. The pupil of an octopus's eye is slit-shaped, and the animal keeps the slit horizontal, no matter what angle its body is at.

Below each eye, near the entrance to the mantle cavity, is a pit containing a chemical sense organ that can sample the water that enters. Each cephalopod also has organs that can detect which way up the animal is in the water. Octopuses seem to have chemical sense cells over much of their surface, so can put out an arm to "taste" something. They also have a good sense of touch, and can distinguish between different textures and types of surface. They are good at picking up and manipulating objects.

CHANGEABLE COLOR

A cephalopod's skin is thin and sensitive. It is also amazingly good at changing color. An octopus can alter instantaneously from one color to another, and color patterns, even the texture of the skin, are changeable. Often the colors are good for camouflage, blending with the tones of the background. But they may also show mood. An octopus about to pounce flushes dark. One that is frightened becomes light colored and flattens itself against rocks. Sometimes waves of color may pass across the skin.

The Common cuttlefish, too, has a dazzling color range. It can be sandy to match the sea bottom, almost colorless, or a variety of shades and patterns, culminating in the zebra stripes of a courting male. Animals like these with good vision can use color signaling with good effect.

▲ ▶ **Two species of cephalopod** The Common octopus **(1)** lives in the Mediterranean area and north to the English Channel. It grows to a maximum of 3ft long overall, but is often smaller. The Common pearly nautilus **(2)** grows about 8in long. Over 30 tentacles protrude from the protective shell when the nautilus is active.

Color change is under the control of the brain. The colors exist in the skin in special pigment cells. Each cell has little muscles attached, so it may be spread wide or become just a pinhead. Pigment cells may have black, reddish, orange, yellow, silvery or other pigments, giving a huge range of possible color combinations.

INVISIBLE WITH INK
Another visual trick can be played by these molluscs. Opening into the mantle cavity is a gland that produces a dark pigment. A quantity of this can be shot out in a little cloud when the animal is alarmed. The cloud is about the same size as the animal itself. As it ejects the pigment, the cuttlefish changes color and shoots away by jet propulsion. An enemy is left looking at the puff of ink, as it is called, while the cuttlefish escapes unnoticed.

Most cephalopods are able to produce ink. In the case of the Common cuttle it quite literally is ink, for the dried glands of these animals used to be ground up and used as writing-ink.

MAKING LIGHT
Many ocean-dwelling squid can produce their own light. They have special light-producing organs, often in bands or patches along the body. Each species has its own patterns and colors. The little squid *Lycoteuthis* has a set of blue, white and red "lights." These probably allow the squids to recognize and signal to one another, and in some cases help camouflage them or lure prey.

FLYING SQUAD
Most of the squids that live near the surface have bodies just slightly denser than sea water. Their movement and the action of their fins keeps

them up. They ripple the fins along the sides of the body and use jet propulsion for movement. A number of species can get up such a speed that they can shoot several feet out of the water to escape enemies. A few can "fly" above the surface for 150ft.

Some cephalopods have special ways of making themselves buoyant. The Common pearly nautilus dives to 2,000ft, but can rise or fall by changing the amount of gas in the chambers of its shell. Cuttlefish can perform a similar buoyancy trick with the gases in their spongy shell.

GIANTS
Generally, cephalopods are small. The majority of squids are less than 12in in length. Most octopuses are about 3ft long and are certainly not man-eaters, but there are some giants. One Pacific octopus can grow to 30ft across with arms spread.

The real giant, though, is the Giant squid, which lives in the sea depths. This can grow to a total length of 65ft to the end of its arms. Such monsters have suckers on the arms that are 12in or more across. Little is known about their habits, but Sperm whales sometimes bear scars that were obviously made by the suckers and beak of Giant squids they tried to eat.

The most buoyant parts of a Giant squid are the arms. This monster of the deep may hang motionless in the water like an upside-down umbrella, waiting for prey.

MATING AT ARM'S LENGTH
In most cephalopods the male is larger than the female, but the reverse is true in all species of octopus. The male cephalopod develops its third arm as an organ for placing a packet of sperm into the female's mantle cavity.

Among octopuses, the two partners mate at arm's length. After this, the eggs are fertilized internally and then shed into the water.

Cephalopod eggs are relatively large and yolky. In the Common cuttlefish, the eggs are laid singly. In the Common squid, they are laid in strings, and all the females in a shoal may lay their eggs close to one another's.

In the Common octopus, up to 150,000 eggs are laid in bunches over a period of about a week, often under the roof of the female's lair. She stays guarding them, washing them with jets of water from her funnel, for some 6 weeks. The eggs hatch as minute octopuses, and the female soon dies. In many cephalopods, both adults die shortly after breeding.

◄ Here it is mating time for a group of squid (*Loligo* species) off the coast of California. A male transfers a packet of sperm with a special arm.

► The Lesser octopus grows 20in long, and has a single row of suckers down each arm. Here an individual has caught a crab, one of its favorite foods.

SPINY-SKINNED ANIMALS

A sea cucumber moves slowly through the beds of eelgrass, gathering its food. A fish spots it, and bites at what looks like a tasty morsel. But the sea cucumber bends the rear of its body towards the attacker and squirts out some thin white sticky threads. The fish recoils from the sudden retaliation. The sea cucumber goes safely on its way.

Sea cucumbers are echinoderms, a distinct animal type that is easily recognizable. The name echinoderm means spiny-skinned, and most members of the phylum have defensive spines on the outside of their bodies. They are found only in the sea, and cannot live in fresh water. As adults, they almost all live on the seabed.

There are five main groups of echinoderm – the sea urchins, the starfish, the brittle stars, the feather stars, and the sea cucumbers. Starfish and brittle stars are dealt with in more detail on pages 78-81, and the sea urchins on pages 82-85. The other groups, and echinoderms in general, are dealt with in this article.

HEADLESS CREATURES
Unusually for such complex animals, echinoderms have no head. Nor do they have a front and back. They are what is known as radially symmetrical, with similar body parts radiating from the center. In most species the body parts are arranged in fives. Most starfish, for example, have five arms. This kind of arrangement is not found, though, in echinoderm larvae, which have two mirror-image sides as in most animals (bilateral symmetry).

PROTECTIVE PLATES
Echinoderms have a hard chalky skeleton that supports the body wall or "test" as it is known. This skeleton is covered by living tissue. In the sea cucumbers, the crystals of the skeleton are embedded in the body wall and are joined by flexible tissue, thus leaving the animal supple. In the feather stars, the skeleton is massive and arranged as a series of plates, ossicles (little bones) and spines, with very little soft tissue. In these animals the main organs are contained in a small cup-shaped body, which has a protective skeleton of plates.

TUBE-FEET AND STALKS
A feature of all echinoderms is a system of water vessels which runs through the body. Originally, this probably served to help with breathing, and it developed little blind-ended sacs that protrude from the body. These water-filled "tube-feet" can be moved about, lengthened or shortened, by muscular action. In the

▲A feather star extends its arms to strain food material from the sea and pass it down grooves lined with hairs.

feather stars, their main use is to gather particles of food suspended in the water. In sea cucumbers and other echinoderms, the tube-feet are also important in moving, and the tips may act as suckers for gripping.

There are about 650 species of feather star and sea lily. Feather stars live in shallower water. Sea lilies were known as fossils before living species were found in the deep sea. They live from about 650ft to 5mi beneath the surface. They spend most of the time attached by stalks to the seabed.

▶Some species of echinoderm
A starfish, *Pisaster ochraceus* (1). A brittle star, *Ophiarachnella incrassata* (2). A sea urchin, *Evechinus chloroticus* (3). A basket star, *Astrobia nuda* (4). Crown-of-thorns starfish, *Acanthaster planci* (5). A sea urchin, *Diadema antillarum* (6). A sea cucumber, *Pseudocolochirus axiologus* (7). A heart urchin, *Spatangus purpureus* (8).

SPINY-SKINNED ANIMALS Phylum
Echinodermata (*6,000 species*)

Habitat: sea water.

Diet: small animals or plants or filter-feed particles of food.

Breeding: sexes generally separate; external fertilization; eggs and larvae planktonic.

Distribution: worldwide.

Size: ⅕in to 3ft across.

Color: very varied.

Species mentioned in text:
Feather star (e.g., *Antedon bifida*)
Sea cucumber (e.g., *Holothuria forskali*)
Sea lily (e.g., *Rhizocrinus lofotensis*)

8

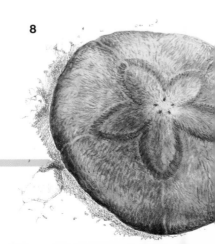

STARFISH

A Common starfish moves into position on a mussel bed. It straddles a large mussel. The starfish takes hold on the ground with some of its suckered tube-feet, and grasps the mussel with others. It then begins to pull. For many minutes the muscle holding the mussel's shell closed shows no signs of weakening, but then the shell begins to gape. The starfish begins another meal.

Some kinds of starfish feed on small edible particles or microscopic organisms, but many are very efficient and persistent predators. They eat animals such as worms, molluscs and other echinoderms. They are able to "smell" the presence of suitable prey in the water and move towards it. The Common starfish feeds on oysters and mussels. These animals at first sight seem protected by their shells, but the starfish gets through their defenses.

STOMACH TURNING

The molluscs are too large to be swallowed, so the starfish uses its grip and pulling power to wrench open their shells. Wrench is perhaps the wrong word for a process that may take more than 20 minutes. Some

starfish have been known to persist with their effort for as long as 2 days.

Once the mollusc's shell is open, the starfish turns out its own stomach and inserts it in the gap between the shells. It then proceeds to digest the mussel's soft tissues. This process may take up to 15 hours. Once the shell is empty, the starfish moves away, perhaps on to its next meal.

If a mollusc is too big, or in too awkward a position for pulling it apart to be possible, then a starfish may be able to insert its stomach through any tiny gap or irregularity in the shells' fit. Sometimes only part of the prey may be reached, and digestion using just part of its stomach may take a starfish even longer than normal.

The sunstars, too, feed on mussels and oysters, but they occasionally also prey on the Common starfish. A sunstar may eat a starfish's arm as the victim is still walking about.

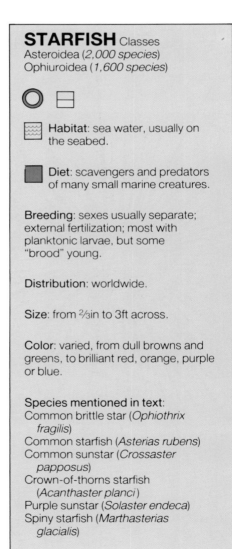

STARFISH Classes
Asteroidea (*2,000 species*)
Ophiuroidea (*1,600 species*)

○ ▢

▨ **Habitat:** sea water, usually on the seabed.

■ **Diet:** scavengers and predators of many small marine creatures.

Breeding: sexes usually separate; external fertilization; most with planktonic larvae, but some "brood" young.

Distribution: worldwide.

Size: from ⅔in to 3ft across.

Color: varied, from dull browns and greens, to brilliant red, orange, purple or blue.

Species mentioned in text:
Common brittle star (*Ophiothrix fragilis*)
Common starfish (*Asterias rubens*)
Common sunstar (*Crossaster papposus*)
Crown-of-thorns starfish (*Acanthaster planci*)
Purple sunstar (*Solaster endeca*)
Spiny starfish (*Marthasterias glacialis*)

▼ The Spiny starfish is a meat-eater, like others of this group. Here one has wrapped its arms round a sea squirt.

◀Between the spines on the arm of this Crown-of-thorns starfish, tube-feet can be clearly seen. Flexible, and filled with water, each ends in a small yellow sucker, giving the arms a powerful grip.

▼The Purple sunstar, a species found off the coasts of northern Europe, does not have the usual five arms. This species usually has 9 or 10 arms, but others have any number from 7 to 13.

CORAL DINER

The tropical Crown-of-thorns starfish is a specialist at eating corals. Unable to swallow chunks of the reef, it everts its stomach and digests the coral polyps that are buried in the reef. It then moves on, leaving the empty coral-skeleton cups behind. Off Australia, it is highly destructive of the Great Barrier Reef.

Some starfish tackle unlikely prey. The very flat Goose-foot star, so called because of the web between its arms, is able to capture active animals such as swimming crabs and shrimps. How this is done is not known. The large starfish *Pycnopodia helianthoides*, which lives off the west coast of North America, grows to nearly 3½ft across and has anything up to 24 arms. It swallows whole hermit crabs and sea urchins, seeming not to mind their shells and spines.

A few starfish of European coasts, such as *Astropecten*, also swallow food whole. Their diet includes anything from microscopic creatures to crustaceans and shellfish. The tube-feet of such starfish have no suckers, so they cannot pull shells apart for digestion outside the body.

GATHERING IN GROUPS

Some starfish are very greedy, eating their own bulk in food in as little as a couple of days. The greediest starfish, however, tend to be those that feed in

groups. When starfish are spaced well apart, their regular feeding is usually moderate, and is performed at night. When a food source is especially good, though, large numbers of starfish may gather in one place. When this happens, the animals seem to stimulate one another to feed more, eating by day as well as night. The individuals in these greedy groups grow larger and faster than normal.

BRITTLE SUCCESS

The brittle stars (class Ophiuroidea) feed on small food particles in the water. They catch these on sticky mucus along their arms, and then cilia (tiny hairs) flick the food down towards the mouth. Some brittle stars live in huge "beds" on the sea bottom, and their combined power to sift the water near the seabed must be very substantial. The brittle star *Amphipholis squamata* occurs in large numbers anywhere from the shore to depths of 800ft. It measures about 2in across. It is one of the most cosmopolitan of animals, being found in seas from America to New Zealand.

CATCHING BASKET
The basket stars have arms like brittle stars, but branched upwards and outwards into a kind of basket-shaped framework that can be 24in across. This forms a very efficient trap for shrimps. When the prey touches the basket, a branch curls in quickly and holds it. The arm then bends to carry the victim to the mouth.

▼ This damaged Common starfish is growing two new arms. Some may lose four arms and still recover.

COLORED STARS
Starfish come in many different colors. The Common starfish is often reddish, hence its species name *rubens*, but it can be yellow, orange or even purple. The Common brittle star is also variable, some individuals being violet or purple, others brown, bright red, or patterned.

Probably reddish colors are most common in starfish as carotenoid pigments (similar to those in carrots and tomatoes) are often present. But there are some startling exceptions, for example the bright blue *Linckia* of the Great Barrier Reef region.

WATERPOWER
In brittle stars, the tube-feet are used for transferring food to the mouth, and are not used much in moving

about. Instead each whole arm bends and moves to help the animals along.

In typical starfish, the tube-feet are important for both moving about and dealing with food. Each tube-foot has a little water reservoir, or ampulla, above it inside the animal's body. The ampulla has its own muscular system, and can squeeze water into the tube-foot to make it extend. In each arm, all the ampullae are joined by a thin water canal that then leads into a main circular "ring" canal around the mouth. This connects to the outside water through a "sieve plate" on the upper surface.

Tube-feet often have suckers, but in some starfish they do not. Generally these are species that burrow in sand.

The water vascular system has other jobs apart from controlling the tube-

◄The Common sunstar, up to 10in wide, lives in the sea among beds of oysters and mussels below the shore in northern Europe.

Starfish larvae have bands of cilia to help them swim; they do not yet have arms. Larval life may be just a few weeks, or months. The majority die from lack of food or being eaten. At the end of this time, in just a few hours, the animal changes to the adult, and it settles on the seabed.

A few species of brittle star have, during evolution, lost the planktonic larva, and the young develop within the disc (body center) of the mother. One of these is the wide-ranging *Amphipholis squamata*. This is unusual in that its eggs are small, unlike those of most brooding species. The young seem to get nourishment from the parent. Another accomplishment of this species is that it is able to make its arms glow in the dark.

BODY REPAIRS

Starfish are able to regenerate (grow again) each of their arms. Some can regenerate their whole body from a single arm. There are even starfish that can reproduce by pulling themselves apart across the middle of the disc. These are usually kinds that normally have more than five arms.

feet. It transports food and waste material, and carries oxygen and carbon dioxide to and from the tissues of the body. It also contains cells that help with excretion and body repairs.

A SENSELESS EXISTENCE?

In a starfish, there is no head and no brain. Nerves run equally to all five arms. When a starfish moves, it may lead with any of its arms, whichever direction it takes. A few species, though, have been observed to have a particular "leading" arm. Some lead with the gap where water enters the vascular system via the sieve plate, which may have a sensory role.

In fact, there seem to be few special sense organs in echinoderms. In starfish, there are rudimentary eyes (optic cushions) at the tip of each arm, and scattered over the body surface are simple touch and chemical (taste/smell) receptor cells. Some scientists believe that all the cells in a starfish's outer skin have a sensory function.

►The flexible arms of brittle stars have many little units called ossicles that fit together like the bones in our spines.

SWIM AND THEN SINK

When breeding, male and female starfish do not come in contact and simply release sperm and eggs directly into the sea. Water temperature, and chemicals produced by the starfish themselves, may stimulate them to spawn at the same time. A Common starfish may lay 2.5 million eggs in one spawning. In most species, the fertilized eggs drift in the plankton, and so too do the larvae that hatch.

SEA URCHINS

A long-spined sea urchin sits on the shelf of a tropical reef. A hunting fish, with powerful beak-like jaws, hovers nearby. As it moves along the reef, its shadow falls on the urchin. Immediately the urchin's long spines swivel so that many of them point upwards to give protection. When the shadow passes, the spines gradually relax.

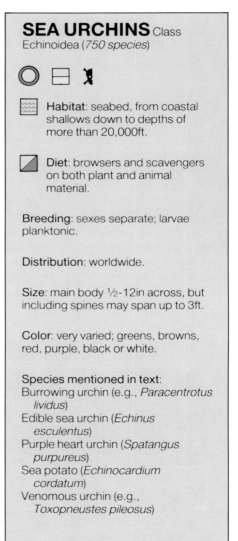

SEA URCHINS Class
Echinoidea (*750 species*)

○ ⊟ 🗡

Habitat: seabed, from coastal shallows down to depths of more than 20,000ft.

Diet: browsers and scavengers on both plant and animal material.

Breeding: sexes separate; larvae planktonic.

Distribution: worldwide.

Size: main body ½-12in across, but including spines may span up to 3ft.

Color: very varied; greens, browns, red, purple, black or white.

Species mentioned in text:
Burrowing urchin (e.g., *Paracentrotus lividus*)
Edible sea urchin (*Echinus esculentus*)
Purple heart urchin (*Spatangus purpureus*)
Sea potato (*Echinocardium cordatum*)
Venomous urchin (e.g., *Toxopneustes pileosus*)

The sea urchins are the spiniest of the spiny-skinned animals (see pages 76-77). Many of them look like a ball covered with spines. Their simple shape disguises complex structures in their skeletons and body coverings.

UPSIDE-DOWN BODY PLAN
The mouth of a sea urchin is in the middle underneath. The anus is at the top. Twenty vertical rows of six-sided bony plates fit together just below the skin to make a tough test (body wall). Running up the test are lines of pores where the tube-feet emerge to the outside. Many urchins have very extensible tube-feet, and they can reach out some distance beyond the spines to steady the animal or help it move.

▲ Sea urchins have rows of tube-feet between the spines. On this species, they can be seen extending to the right.

PIN-CUSHIONS AND FUR COATS
The spines of sea urchins are set on hard knobs on the test. In some urchins, such as *Cidaris* species, the knobs are especially large, and so are the spines. Forms within the genus *Diadema* may have spines 12in long. In most urchins, though, the spines are less than half the width of the test, and the covering is uniformly bristly.

Perhaps the oddest spines are those of the tropical *Heterocentrotus* species, which have thick triangular spines. They use them to wedge in crevices while resting during the hours of

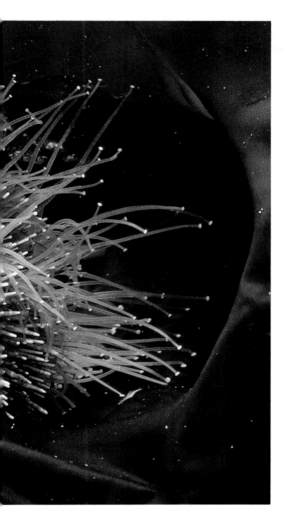

▶Skeleton of a sand dollar *Mellita testudinata* washed up on a beach; normally they live buried in sand.

daylight. These urchins emerge at night to feed on algae.

The opposite extreme is found in some of the heart urchins, in which the spines lie almost flat and form a covering that looks like a fur coat.

The spines are often important in movement. Movement with tube-feet is sure, but very slow. Some sea urchins can climb vertical rocks by holding on with them. However, the highest speed attained in movement on the flat is 33ft per hour. Using the spines as stilts for walking, some sea urchins go at ten times that rate.

ODD ONES OUT

The globular urchins show perfect five-rayed symmetry. Heart urchins and their relations, though, have developed, for echinoderms, an odd sort of symmetry. In these animals the mouth is set forward, and the anus back, so that they have two mirror-image halves. When heart urchins move, the mouth-end leads. The flattened species known as sand dollars are burrowers that plough through the sand, front first, finding food as they go. Tiny particles of food are passed to the mouth by tube-feet or along rows of sticky cilia (small hairs).

EATING THROUGH THE SAND

Heart urchins, such as the Sea potato, dig themselves down into the sand using the spines on their sides. It can be a slow process. Once buried, they move forward slowly. These animals use long tube-feet to keep open a mucus-lined tube up to the surface so it is easy for them to breathe. This tube may be up to 8in long. The heart urchins replace it constantly as they travel along. They also use tube-feet to keep open temporarily a tube in the sand behind them, through which they push out waste from the gut.

Heart urchins swallow the sand as they go, removing edible particles as it travels through the gut, and passing "clean" sand out of the anus.

ROCK-BURROWERS

Some of the globular sea urchins also burrow, but into rock not sand. They make a hole in the rock with their spines and teeth. A species that lives in the southern Pacific creates burrows several inches deep. It spends most

▲ The Edible sea urchin is caught for its roe (egg masses) off Britain and Portugal. Other species are considered delicacies in other parts of the world.

of its time at the entrance, but is able to fall back into the burrow when disturbed, wedging itself with some spines and directing others towards any potential attacker.

A LIGHT DIET?

The ordinary globular sea urchins have a complicated set of jaws in their mouths. An internal bony framework ends in five sharp teeth. The whole jaw skeleton is called an Aristotle's lantern, because of its resemblance to an old lamp. It is used by most species for grazing on, and crunching up, bottom-living algae and static animals such as barnacles and sponges.

These urchins may also collect food particles on their upper body surfaces. They are passed to the mouth by tube-feet, spines, or the grooming organs known as pedicellariae.

USEFUL TONGS

Pedicellariae are found between the spines of sea urchins. Some starfish have them too, but theirs are not so well developed. Each of these organs has a flexible stalk. At the top is a set of tiny jaws or tongs. If an intruder such as a tiny crustacean settles on an urchin's test, it causes the tongs to gape open. If the tongs are touched, they snap shut, trapping the intruder. The tongs can keep the surface of the urchin clear of parasites and other unwanted arrivals.

Several sea urchins' tongs have evolved one stage further and possess venom (poison) sacs. The jaws close only on objects that have certain chemicals the urchins "recognize." Venom is injected via a hollow tooth-like structure. In some species, the venom has a powerful effect. The top section of the tongs comes off when venom is injected and remains in the tissue of an intruder. These pedicellariae are used mainly by the sea urchins as defenses against such large predators as starfish.

CREATURES OF THE DEEP

Some sea urchins are found at considerable depths. The Purple heart urchin, which is often seen on the lower shore, can be found down to 3,300ft. Tracks of similar urchins have been seen 13,000ft beneath the surface. Some of the largest sea urchins live at depths of at least 20,000ft. Many appear beautifully colored reds and violets when illuminated.

◄On reefs in the tropics, sea urchins of the genus *Diadema* have exceptionally long sharp spines. These are hollow, and may break off in an attacker's skin.

SEA SQUIRTS

Attached to a rock sits a group of small animals. Their transparent bodies look at first sight like lifeless jelly. But when one is touched, it contracts violently, shooting out water from its body. These are adult sea squirts. There is little to suggest that these animals are some of our closest relations among the invertebrates.

Chordates are "higher" animals that have a single, hollow nerve cord along their backs, with a stiffening rod, or notochord, below it. The most familiar chordates are the vertebrates – fish, amphibians, reptiles, birds and mammals – where the notochord has, in the adults, developed into the bony backbone. But in the sea live animals such as sea squirts which have basic chordate characteristics.

WATER PUMPS
Adult sea squirts grow attached to rocks or other organisms. The outside of the body is a thick coat made of a substance similar to the cellulose of plant cell walls. At the top of the body is a hole (the inlet siphon), and at the side is an outlet one.

The animals pump water into the middle of their bodies, through their basket-like gills, and then squirt it away via their outlet siphons. The gills extract oxygen, and also filter out food from the water. The gills have cilia (hairs) which are moved constantly to keep the current flowing. The gut, heart and sex organs, both male and female, lie below the gills.

ALONE AND IN GROUPS
Some species of sea squirt live alone. Others live jumbled loosely together with individuals of their own kind. A few, for example the Star sea squirt, form colonies in which a distinct group of individuals have a common outlet siphon, but bear their own inlet siphons. These groups form little colored "stars" within a flattened jelly-like colony that develops as a thin crust on a rock.

In some sea squirts, at breeding time eggs and sperm are simply shed into the sea and fertilization is external. Other species keep the sex cells, the fertilized eggs and all the early embryos within the body.

A WRIGGLING TADPOLE
So far in the sea squirt life cycle there is little to suggest a relationship with vertebrates, but this changes when the larva develops.

In just a few hours or days after fertilization, the embryo develops into a tadpole-like larva. The tadpole is

▼ Sea squirts growing in a colony on the Great Barrier Reef off Australia. In some species the green coloring is due to algae that grow in the animal's tissues.

SEA SQUIRTS Subphylum
Urochordata (*2,000 species*)

Habitat: seas, both bottom-living and floating forms.

Diet: filter-feeders.

Breeding: each animal both male and female; tadpole-like swimming larvae.

Distribution: worldwide.

Size: individuals ½-8in long.

Color: varied colors, or transparent.

Species mentioned in text:
Star sea squirt (*Botryllus schlosseri*)

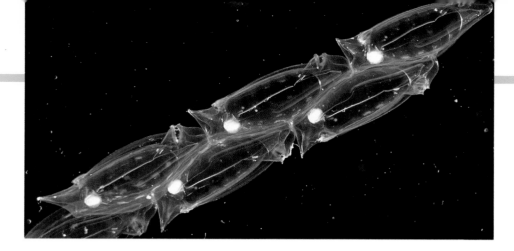

▲ Like a row of glass bottles, these colonial salps drift through the deep waters of the ocean. They eat small plankton filtered out by their gills.

▼ Living up to their name, these red colonial sea squirts on a rocky shore in South Africa send jets of water squirting into the air.

able to swim, and is sensitive to light and gravity. It can move to select a suitable site to settle and turn into a bag-like adult. For a brief period, though, it is an independent animal, with a hollow nerve cord, and a notochord to stiffen the tail and give something for the tail muscles to pull on as it wiggles on its way. After a few days, the "infant" attaches to a rock, and stays put for the rest of its life.

SALPS

Related to sea squirts are the salps. These are transparent barrel-shaped animals that swim near the surface of the sea. In some parts of the sea they live in huge numbers. They pulsate as they swim, taking planktonic food into the body. Some kinds live as individuals. Others may be found in large colonies strung through the water. Once again, these appear to be simple animals, but at some stage in the life cycle they have tadpole-like larvae like those of the sea squirts.

Oikopleura is another relative. It is a tiny creature that keeps the tadpole shape and a stiffened muscular swimming tail throughout its life. It uses this tail to help draw water through the openings of the jelly "house" that it secretes round its body.

LANCELETS

A Chinese fisherman pulls in his net. It is full of small shiny fish-shaped creatures. These are not fish, though. They are invertebrates called lancelets. They resemble the ancestors of vertebrates (mammals, birds, fish and so on) from millions of years ago. But this does not matter to the fisherman. These creatures are good to eat, and he collects them from his net.

LANCELETS Subphylum Cephalochordata (*20 species*)

Habitat: sea bottom.

Diet: filter-feeder, extracting animal and plant material from the water.

Breeding: sexes separate; larvae planktonic.

Distribution: temperate and tropical seas; in scattered clusters.

Size: length up to 2in.

Color: semi-transparent with an overall pinkish or purplish tinge.

Species mentioned in text:
Common lancelet (*Branchiostoma lanceolatum*)

Lancelets were first described scientifically, and named *Branchiostoma*, by the Russian naturalist Pallas in 1778, but he thought they were some sort of mollusc (snail-like animal). In 1836 they were rediscovered by another scientist, who gave them the name *Amphioxus*, and noticed the stiffening rod, or notochord, running down their back inside the body. The name amphioxus stuck, and although by the rules among scientists the earlier *Branchiostoma* must be the correct scientific name, amphioxus is often used as a sort of alternative common name.

It is not surprising that early naturalists did not appreciate the true nature of these animals, which show some similarities to the vertebrates, yet still have no real head or backbone.

UNDERGROUND FILTER

Lancelets are so called because of their flat blade-like shape. They have no paired fins, but there is a trace of a tail fin and a ridge along the back and under the tail supported by gelatinous fin rays. Obvious blocks of muscle run down the length of the animal.

The Common lancelet spends most of its time buried in sand or fine gravel on the sea floor. The tail and most of the body is below the surface, but the front end protrudes above it. At the very front is a "hood" over the top of a ring of little tentacles around the mouth, where the animal sucks in a current of water. The tentacles filter out large particles and stop them going into the mouth. Water and small food particles enter the mouth and are passed through the gills. A pouch surrounds the gills, and at the rear of this is a single opening that provides an exit for water.

There are a large number of gill slits for the water to pass through. The gills obtain oxygen and get rid of carbon dioxide, but they are also important filtering devices to take suspended particles out of the water, including tiny plants. There are many cilia (hairs) on the gills, and they pass food to a ciliated gutter below. Here the food is wrapped in mucus and passed to the gut for digestion. The beating cilia keep up an almost continuous current through the gills.

ANIMAL FROM THE PAST

Although superficially fish-like, lancelets lack many fish features, and have some peculiar ones of their own. The notochord runs from the very front to the back of each animal. The hollow nerve cord above this does not stretch quite as far, but it sends off branches to supply the muscles and other organs. The blocks of muscle on each side of the notochord run down most of the animal's length, like the blocks of muscle along a fish's backbone. They allow it to swim quite strongly when it does emerge from the sand.

In lancelets there is nothing that could be called a brain. There are also no skull, no jaws, no true eyes or other sense organs that would be found in vertebrates. There is just a light-sensitive spot at the front of the body. There is no heart, but a pulsating vessel drives the colorless blood through the gills and around the body.

Many of the lancelets' features are those that might be expected in a primitive ancestor of vertebrates. In fact, in rocks 550 million years old, from a time before there were fish, fossils have been found of an animal looking much like the lancelets.

REPRODUCTION

The sex organs of a lancelet consist of a series of distinct oval pouches running beneath the muscle blocks. They may be visible as creamy colored organs in the living animal.

Sperm or eggs are released into the water, where fertilization occurs. A swimming larva develops that has a form unlike the adult's. For several months, as it feeds and matures, it lies on the seabed during the day and swims to join the plankton at night. When it reaches about ⅕in long, it becomes an adult.

▶Two lancelets lie in typical posture, with tails buried in the gravel and heads protruding. The sheen of the muscle blocks along each side of the body can be seen through the skin. Lancelets use their muscles to swim actively.

GLOSSARY

Abdomen The rear section of the body, especially in such animals as crustaceans.

Adaptation Any feature of an animal that fits it to live in its surroundings.

Adult A sexually mature, but not necessarily full-sized, individual capable of breeding.

Antennae A pair of head appendages carrying sense organs.

Appendage A body attachment such as a leg or antenna.

Aquatic Living for much, if not all of the time, in water.

Asexual reproduction A means of producing offspring without the fusion of sex cells (sperm and eggs) and usually by splitting or budding of the body.

Backbone A column of interlinked bones, the vertebrae, which forms the spine of animals such as fish and mammals. Invertebrates do not have a backbone.

Bilateral symmetry A form of proportions in which the body consists of a central axis running from head to tail either side of which similar parts are arranged in a mirror-image fashion, as in worms and crabs.

Bivalve A shell or protective covering composed of two parts hinged together enclosing the body, as in a bivalve mollusc.

Brood pouch A special body sac or pouch in an adult in which eggs and young are carried before being released into the outside world.

Budding A form of asexual reproduction in which a new individual develops as a direct growth from the body of the parent.

Carapace A shell that covers the top of the body, as that in crabs.

Carnivorous Describes an animal that feeds on other animals, its prey.

Cephalothorax The combined head (cephalo) and front region (thorax) of the body, fused together in animals such as crabs and lobsters.

Chaetae The bristles protruding from the skin of annelid worms.

Chordate An animal that possesses a notochord, belonging to the Phylum Chordata.

Cilia (singular, cilium) The tiny hair-like projections from the surface of some cells and single-celled animals. Cilia are able to beat in waves.

Colony An organism consisting of a number of individuals that live together permanently.

Cyst A resting stage of a cell, larva or organism enclosed in a thick-walled protective membrane.

Display An easy-to-see pattern of behavior that conveys information to other animals, such as readiness to mate.

Distribution The whole area in the world in which a species is found.

External fertilization Joining of eggs and sperm outside the female's body.

Filter-feeding A method of feeding in which small pieces of food, or tiny animals and plants, are extracted from water by a part of the animal that acts as a sieve.

Flagellum (plural flagella) A long, fine thread, sticking out from a cell and moving in a lashing or waving fashion.

Free-living Able to wander at will; refers to animals not fixed to a particular spot.

Genus The division of animal classification below Family and above Species.

Gill The breathing organ of an aquatic animal. In some species, gills are also used in feeding to filter food from the water.

Habitat The surroundings in which an animal lives, including the plant life, other animals, physical surroundings and climate.

Hermaphrodite Describes an animal in which both male and female reproductive organs are present.

Internal fertilization Joining of eggs and sperm inside the body of the female.

Introduced Living in an area as a result of being taken there, deliberately or accidentally, by people, rather than spreading naturally.

Invertebrate Any animal that does not have a backbone, such as a worm or a snail.

Larva A young stage of an animal between egg and adult.

Mantle A fold of skin covering all or part of the body in molluscs; its outer edge secretes the shell.

Mantle cavity The cavity between mantle and body in a mollusc; it often contains the breathing organs.

Marine Living in the sea.

Medusa The free-swimming "jellyfish" sexual stage in the life cycle of sea anemones and their relatives.

Migration Movement, usually seasonal, from one region to another for the purpose of feeding or breeding.

Mucus Sticky, slimy substance produced by some animals on their skin or membranes lining their digestive systems.

Nematocyst A stinging cell found characteristically in cnidarians such as jellyfish and sea anemones.

Notochord A stiffening rod that extends down the back of certain animals at some stage in their life histories. Animals with a notochord are known as chordates. In vertebrates it is the forerunner of the backbone.

Omnivorous Describes an animal which includes both plant and animal material in its diet.

Organic material Material derived from living or dead animals and plants. Being rich in nutrients, it forms the diet of all animals.

Pedicellariae Tiny pincer-like defensive and grooming structures on the body of sea urchins and starfish.

Phylum The first (highest) division of animal classification. All animals with the same basic body plan are put into one phylum. There are 39 phyla in the animal kingdom only one of which, Chordata, includes all the animals with a backbone – the fish, amphibians, reptiles, birds and mammals. Each phylum is divided into one or more Classes of animal.

Pigment A substance that gives color to an animal's body.

Plankton Drifting or swimming animals and plants, many tiny or microscopic, which are carried by water currents due to their limited powers of movement.

Polyp The type of body possessed by sea anemones and corals. A hollow tubular body is connected to the ground at one end. At the other end is a mouth surrounded by tentacles.

Predator Any animal that hunts, catches and kills another animal for food.

Proboscis A tubular organ of many invertebrates that can be extended from the mouth for feeding purposes.

Protozoan A single-celled organism with animal-like characteristics.

Radial symmetry A form of proportions in which the body consists of a central axis around which similar parts are arranged in a regular pattern, as in sea urchins.

Radula The type of tongue found in many molluscs, with many small "teeth" like a file.

Ray A division of the body of an echinoderm, such as a starfish arm.

Sedentary Not moving about. A sedentary organism is usually fixed to one spot, such as a barnacle to a rock.

Segment A unit of an animal's body, repeated down the length of the organism so that it is made up of many similar segments.

Siphon A tube through which water enters or leaves the body of an animal.

Solitary Living alone; refers to animals not permanently with others of their kind.

Species The division of animal classification below Genus; a group of organisms of the same structure that can breed with one another.

Terrestrial Living on land.

Test A shell or thick coat that covers such invertebrates as echinoderms and sea squirts. The test is just beneath the outer skin.

Thorax The "chest" region of an animal, in crustaceans the section between the head and the abdomen.

Tissue A distinct group of cells of the same sort and with the same job.

Tube-feet The hollow water-filled organs of echinoderms used mainly for movement.

Vertebrate Any animal that has a backbone, such as a bird or a fish.

INDEX

sea lilies 76
Sea mouse **30**, 32
Sea potato 84
sea squirt
  Star 86
sea squirts 86-87
  red colonial **87**
  see also salps, sea squirt
sea urchins **76**, 82-85
  see also sand dollar, Sea
    potato, sea urchin, urchin,
    urchins
sea whips 22
shell
  Helmet **61**
  Razor 69
shells
  cone 61, 63
  necklace 63
  triton 63
  see also shell
shipworm 69
shrimp
  Banded cleaner **44**, 45
  Brown 42, 43
  Red 43
shrimps 42-45
  anemone **44**
  brine 37
  cleaner 45
  fairy 37
  freshwater 38
  mantis 42, 44, 45

seed- see ostracod
  tropical 45
  see also krill, prawns, shrimp
Sipunculans 24, 25
slater
  Sea 38, **39**
slug
  Banana **62**
slugs 9, 60-65
  land 63, 65
  sea 61, 63, 65
  shelled 65
  see also gastropods, slug
snail
  African land 65
  Garden 61, 62, 65
  Murex 60
  Roman **61**, 65
snails 8, 60-65
  freshwater 61, 65
  land 61, 62, 65
  sea 61, 62, 65
  see also gastropods, snail
spiny-skinned animals 76-77
sponge
  Bath 14
  Caribbean 15
  Caribbean fire 15
sponges 8, 14-15
  see also sponge
squid
  Giant 9, 74
squids 6, 70-75

see also squid
star
  brittle see brittle stars
  feather see feather stars
starfish 9, 76, 78-81
  Common 78, **80**, 81
  Crown-of-thorns **76**, **79**
  Goose-foot 79
  Spiny **78**
sunstar
  Common **81**
  Purple **79**
sunstars 78
  see also sunstar

tapeworm
  beef 26
  Dog 26
  Pork 26
tapeworms 26
  see also tapeworm
tellin
  Blunt 68
tubeworms 31, 33

urchin
  Edible sea **84**
  Purple heart 85
urchins
  burrowing 84
  globular 84
  heart 83, 84
  venomous 85

whelk
  Dog 60, **64**
  European **64**
whelks 60, 61, 63
  dog 63
  see also whelk
winkles 65
woodlice 38-39
  see also gribble; hog-louse;
    pillbug; slater, Sea;
    woodlouse
woodlouse
  Common European **39**
worm
  Australian giant 29
  Green leaf 30
  Paddle 30
  Palolo 30, 31
  South African giant 29
worms 9, 24-25
  acorn 24
  beard 24
  horsehair 24, 25
  polychaete 30-33
  segmented see annelids
  spiny-headed 24
  see also earthworms,
    echiurans, fanworms,
    flatworms, leeches,
    priapulans, ragworms
    round-worms,
    scaleworms, sipunculans,
    tubeworms

Scientific names

The first name of each
double-barrel Latin name refers
to the *Genus*, the second to the
species. Single names not in
italic refer to a family or
sub-family and are cross
referenced to the Common
name index.

Acanthaster planci
  (Crown-of-thorns starfish)
  76, 79
Acanthocephala phylum
  (spiny-headed worms) 24
Achatina species (African land
  snail) 65
Acineta (protozoan) 12
Acropora species (staghorn
  corals) 20, 23
Actinia equina (Beadlet
  anemone) 17, 18, 19
Actinophrys (protozoan) 12
Actinosphaerium (protozoan)
  10
Adamsia carcinopados (sea
  anemone) 51
Alcyonium digitatum (Dead
  man's fingers) 19
Alpheus species (snapping
  prawns) 43, 44

Amoeba 8, 9, 10
Amphioxus (lancelet) 88
Amphipoda order see
  sandhoppers
Amphipholis squamata (brittle
  star) 79, 81
Anomura infraorder see crabs,
  hermit
Antedon bifida (feather star) 76
Anthozoa class see corals
Anthipathes subpinnata (black
  coral) 22
Aphrodite aculeata (sea mouse)
  30, 32
Aplysina lacunosa (sponge) 15
Arcella (protozoan) 10
Aplysia species (sea hare) 64
Archachatina marginata (large
  African snail) 65
Archidoris pseudoargus (sea
  lemon) 65
Architeuthis harveyi (Giant
  squid) 9, 74
Ariolimax californicus (Banana
  slug) 62
Armadillidium vulgare (pill bug)
  38
Arenicola marina (lugworm) 31,
  32
Artemia species (brine shrimps)
  37
Ascaris lumbricoides (Intestinal
  roundworm) 24

Asellus species (hog-louse)
  38
Astacidea infraorder see
  lobsters, crayfish
Astacus
  astacus (European crayfish)
    48
  fluviatilis (Red crayfish) 48
  pallipes (crayfish) 48
Asterias rubens (Common
  starfish) 78, 80, 81
Asteroidea class see starfish
Astropecten (starfish) 79
Astroboa nuda (basket star)
  76
Aurelia aurita (Common
  jellyfish) 16, 18, 19

Balanus species (Acorn
  barnacle) 40
Birgus latro (Coconut crab) 53
Bivalvia class see bivalves,
  clams, mussels
Botryllus schlosseri (Star sea
  squirt) 86
Brachyura infraorder see
  crabs
Branchellion species (fish leech)
  34
Branchiostoma lanceolatum
  (Common lancelet) 88
Branchipus species (fairy
  shrimps) 37

Buccinum undatum (European
  whelk) 64
Bythograea thermydron (Blind
  crab) 54

Calanus species (marine
  copepods) 37
Caligus species (sea copepods)
  37
Calliactis parasitica (sea
  anemone) 53
Cancer pagurus (Edible crab)
  57
Carcinus maenas (Common
  shore crab) 54, 57
Cardisoma guanhami (Blue land
  crab) 56
Cephalochordata subphylum
  see lancelets
Cephalopoda see cuttlefish,
  octopus, squid
Chaetopterus variopedatus
  (ragworm) 25
Charonia nodifera (triton shell)
  63
Chrysaora hyoscella (Compass
  jellyfish) 17
Cidaris species (sea urchin)
  82
Cirripedia class see barnacles
Clitellata class see earthworms
Cnidaria phylum see jellyfish,
  sea anemones

FURTHER READING

Alexander, R. McNeill (ed) (1986), *The Encyclopedia of Animal Biology*, Facts On File, New York.
Banister, K. and Campbell, A. (eds) (1985), *The Encyclopedia of Aquatic Life*, Facts On File, New York.
Barnes, R.D. (1982), *Invertebrate Zoology*, 4th edn, Holt-Saunders, Philadelphia.
Barrington, E.J.W. (1982), *Invertebrate Structure and Function*, Van Nostrand Reinhold, New York.
Berry, R.J. and Hallam, A. (eds) (1986), *The Encyclopedia of Animal Evolution*, Facts On File, New York.
Bliss, D.E. (ed) (1982-), *The Biology of the Crustacea*, vols 1-10, Academic Press, London and New York.
Cheng, T.C. (1973), *General Parasitology*, Academic Press, New York.

Dakin, W.J. (1952), *Australian Seashores*, Angus and Robertson, Sydney and London.
Grzimek, B. (ed), *Grzimek's Animal Life Encyclopedia* vols 1 and 3, Van Nostrand Reinhold, New York.
Moore, P.D. (ed) (1986), *The Encyclopedia of Animal Ecology*, Facts On File, New York.
Rickets, E.F. and Calvin, J. (1960), *Between Pacific Tides* (3rd edn), Stanford University Press, Palo Alto.
Russell-Hunter, W.D. (1979), *A Life of Invertebrates*, Macmillan, New York, Collier Macmillan, London.
Slater, P.J.B. (ed) (1986), *The Encyclopedia of Animal Behavior*, Facts On File, New York.
Yonge, C.M. and Thompson, T.E. (1976), *Living Marine Molluscs*, Collins, London.

ACKNOWLEDGMENTS

Picture credits

Key: *t* top. *b* bottom. *c* center. *l* left. *r* right.
Abbreviations: A Ardea. AN Agence Nature. ANT Australasian Nature Transparencies. BCL Bruce Coleman Ltd. NHPA Natural History Photographic Agency. NSP Natural Science Photos. OSF Oxford Scientific Films. P Premaphotos. PEP Planet Earth Pictures. SAL Survival Anglia Ltd. SPL Science Photo Library

6 OSF/P. Parks. 8*t* NHPA. 8*b* Heather Angel. 9*t* NHPA/S. Dalton. 9*b* C. Howson. 12 BCL/K. Taylor. 13 OSF/P. Parks. 14 NHPA/B. Wood. 15 OSF. 16 NSP/I. Bennett & F. Myers. 17*t* OSF/G. Bernard. 17*b* PEP/P. Atkinson. 20 BCL. 21 PEP/Warren Williams. 22 NHPA/B. Wood. 23*t,b* OSF/F. Ehrenström. 25 Biofotos/H. Angel. 26 OSF/P. Parks. 27 B. Picton. 28 P. 29 NHPA/S. Dalton. 30 A/P. Morris. 31*t* NHPA/B. Wood. 31*b* OSF/A. Kuiter. 35*tl* SPL/M. Dohrn. 35*tr* ANT/R. & D. Keller. 35*b* BCL/K. Taylor. 37*t* AN/Chaumeton. 37*b* NHPA/G. Bernard. 38 BCL/K. Taylor. 39 P. 40-41 OSF/D. Shale. 43*t,b* NSP/I. Bennett. 44*t* A/V. Taylor. 44*b* NHPA. 46-47 OSF. 47 BCL/R. Schroeder. 48 SAL/L. & T. Bomford. 50 BCL/R. Williams. 51 A. Bannister. 52-53 Biofotos/Heather Angel. 54 ANT/Keith Davey. 55*t* BCL/C.B. Frith. 55*b* PEP/D. Maitland. 56*t* NHPA/J. Carmichael. 56-57 A. 58 OSF. 59*t* BCL. 59*b* Biofotos/H. Angel. 60 P. 61*t* OSF/G. Bernard. 61*b* NSP/I. Bennett. 62*t* Biophoto Associates. 62*b* PEP/K. Lucas. 63*t* PEP/C. Pétron. 63*b* B. Picton. 64 OSF/R. Kuiter. 65 A/V. Taylor. 66*c* Biofotos/H. Angel. 66*b* Biofotos/S. Summerhays. 67 PEP/F. Jackson. 68 OSF/J. Cooke. 69 OSF/G. Bernard. 70-71 PEP/K. Lucas. 72*t* PEP/W. Deas. 72*b* B. Picton. 74 BCL. 75 A/P. Morris. 76 NHPA/A. Bannister. 78 C. Howson. 79*t* NHPA/B. Wood. 79*b* C. Howson. 80 P. 81*t* C. Howson. 81*b* PEP/B. Wood. 82-83 OSF/G. Bernard. 83 BCL/J. Shaw. 84 B. Picton. 85 BCL/B Wood. 86 OSF/D. Shale. 87*t* OSF/P. Parks. 87*b* A. Bannister. 89 H. Angel.

Artwork credits.

Key: *t* top. *b* bottom. *c* center. *l* left. *r* right.
Abbreviations ML Mick Loates. RG Roger Gorringe. SD Simon Driver

6, 7, 8 Hayward Art Group. 10 SD. 10-11 RG. 12 SD. 18-19 RG. 24 SD. 25 RG. 26, 27, 28 SD. 29 Keith Shannon. 32-33 RG. 34, 34-35 SD. 36 ML. 39 Linden Artists, Andy Male. 40 ML. 42 SD. 45 Linden Artists, Andy Male. 48-49, 49, 51 ML. 57 Linden Artists, Andy Male. 73 ML. 77 RG.